D0552794

Adventure Sports

MOUNTAIN BIKING

Adventure Sports

MOUNTAIN BIKING

JOHN OLSEN

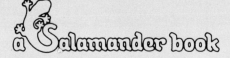

a Salamander book

Published by Salamander Books Limited
LONDON • NEW YORK

A SALAMANDER BOOK

© 1989 Salamander Books Ltd.,
129/137 York Way,
Camden, London, N7 9LG

ISBN 0-86101-457-X

Distributed in the UK by
Hodder & Stoughton Services,
PO Box 6, Mill Road,
Dunton Green, Sevenoaks, Kent
TN13 2XX

All rights reserved. No part of this
book may be reproduced, stored in
a retrieval system or transmitted
by any means, electronic,
mechanical, photocopying,
recording or by information
storage and retrieval system,
without permission of Salamander
Books Ltd. All correspondence
concerning the content of this
volume should be addressed to
Salamander Books Ltd.

Edited by: Bob Munro, Tony Hall
Designed by: Oxprint Ltd

Typeset by: Oxprint Ltd
Artwork by: Oxford Illustrators Ltd
Color reproductions by: Magnum
Graphics Ltd
Printed in Italy

The author
John Olsen has been riding, designing, building, and writing
about mountain bikes since 1981. One of the pioneers of bicycle
trials competition in the United States, he built his first off-road
bicycle (a modified Phillips 3-speed with 1:1 gearing and a front
suspension) in 1968. After a brief off-road cycling hiatus spent
racing motorcycles and getting Bachelor's and Master's
degrees in Mechanical Engineering from Cornell University, Mr.
Olsen went to work for Honda R&D, Ltd., followed by stints at
Boeing Commercial Airplane Co. and a military vehicle company.
Mr. Olsen currently works as a CAE expert, vehicle dynamicist,
cartoonist, and senior test engineer at the PACCAR Technical
Center, working on Peterbilt, Kenworth, and Foden trucks. He has
written about mountain and road bicycles for most of the bicycle
magazines in the U.S., including Bicycling, Bicycle Guide, Bicycle
Rider, Bike Tech, American Bicyclist and Motorcyclist, and
Mountain and City Biking. He currently writes a column for
Mountain and City Biking, focusing on trials, technical trail riding
issues and techniques, humor, and the odd bit of mountain
biking science fiction. Mr. Olsen is an avid mountain trail rider,
and is frequently found riding his own odd bicycles up the
snarliest trails in the foothills of the Cascade mountain range of
western Washington state, where he makes his home with his
lovely wife Valerie, his trials dog Fuzz, two cats, and a cockatiel
who spells better than he does. He was a top-rated expert in
bicycle trials competition until, as he puts it, "them damn kids got
into it, with this freaky hopping stuff!" Nowadays, he is often seen
lurking around trials sections with arcane measuring devices and
physics texts, apparently attempting to figure a way for old age
and technology to overcome youth and skill.

PUBLISHERS NOTE
The sport described in this book is
an inherently dangerous activity and
any person, especially if
inexperienced, undertaking it,
should approach it with caution and
under appropriate supervision. The
publisher cannot accept
responsibility for any accidents,
injury, or loss suffered by any reader
of this book however that may be
caused.

CONTENTS

INTRODUCTION

If you thought that the sport of cycling consisted solely of road racing machines, with their distinctive dropped handle-bars and smooth, skinny tires, the rider hunched forward and pedaling flat out, it's time to think again. While the road racers are still a common sight, a new type of bike has flourished within the world of cycling, taking the rider off the smooth road surfaces to face a new set of cycling challenges. These light, rugged, multi-geared machines, with their fat, knobby tires, have virtually taken over the bicycle market in North America, and are now doing so around the world. The prowess of these machines in the off-road environment is amply reflected in their most common name: the mountain bike.

However, that generic name is slightly misleading, for these bikes are nothing if not versatile. Though they are in their element when pitted against the type of terrain that would quickly defeat any other cycle, mountain bikes are employed in many differing roles: commuting through pot-holed city streets; casual Sunday afternoon rides; heavy touring; quiet rides along beautiful trails; as well as all sorts of intense competition and racing. The mountain bike is a splendidly capable and versatile tool, and it is fair to say that if a person could have only one bicycle, this is by far the best choice.

And yet, there are several different types of mountain bike. A machine designed to do well in one aspect of the sport may not fare so well in another – specialization is starting to emerge. This means that the potential mountain bike buyer must try to answer several important questions: "What type of riding will I be doing most often?" "What type of bike should I buy for that type of riding?" "How will I recognize the right type of bike when I see it?" Mountain bike riding in the true "mountain" sense also requires a combination of good physical fitness and a large body of bike-handling skills.

Don't be put off by the various questions and requirements: this book provides the answers and guidance you will need. Rather than devoting the bulk of the book to mundane mechanical issues (how to adjust your derailleurs, straighten your wheels and tie your shoe laces), the emphasis in the Chapters ahead is on those practical issues that keep most mountain bike riders from getting the most enjoyment and fulfillment from their bikes: buying the right bike; getting into shape to ride it; learning and refining the basic off-road skills; taking those skills into competition.

Mountain bike riding can be the finest sport in the world. It offers an infinite variety of physical and mental challenges, combined with an opportunity to get back into, and fully experience, the woods, streams, hills and mountains in a unique way. But just because other types of bicycles cannot stand up to the rigours of such environments doesn't mean that such areas are our exclusive domain. Conflicts with other users such as hikers and horse riders have the potential to kill the sport of mountain biking. With that in mind, we have included a Chapter explaining how you can avoid such conflicts, and so help our sport flourish.

As you read this book and try the various skill exercises, bear in mind that you will not learn these moves overnight. Patience is absolutely vital. If you are willing to devote the time and effort required, you will be rewarded with the ability to enjoy off-road mountain bike riding to its full. So read on, and enjoy!

John Olsen

CHAPTER 1

THE BIKE

Ten years ago, all mountain bikes were built as general purpose machines. Frame angles were slacker, wheelbases longer, and the riding positions more upright than on today's models. However, mountain biking is a fine example of racing greatly improving the breed, and yesterday's hot racer is today's well-loved general purpose machine. Just as the world of road cycling has its range of specialised designs (touring, racing, track and street bikes), so a variety of special mountain bikes have evolved to meet a diverse range of riding styles and conditions.

The way a person rides a mountain bike is a function of his or her temperament and environment. Some crave the thrill of an all-out, high-speed descent; some seek a challenge to their skill posed by a difficult trail; for others, riding the bike around the neighborhood is just a pleasant form of exercise. Unfortunately, no single bike covers the whole range of riding possibilities. A bike that is optimized for high-speed riding on relatively smooth surfaces like logging roads is not going to do well on a tight, slippery course littered with obstacles. Nor is the perfect woods bike

going to feel right when sliding through corners on a rough desert **fire road** at 30 mph (48 kph.) To some extent you need to know what type of riding you will be doing, and what the riding conditions will be like, before you can make the right choice of mountain bike.

The origins of mountain biking lie in fast descents on steep fire roads and rough trails. Today's mountain bikes have the strength and stability needed to meet the most challenging of off-road and on road surfaces.

Left: Technical Trail riding is an immense challenge to both rider and bike. The lowered top-tube on this machine offers the rider some extra clearance should the going get too rough.

Below: High up in the mountains, a rider turns into a descent on a narrow trail. Slow-speed riding skills and plenty of stamina are essential requirements for these Technical Trail rides.

RIDING STYLES

Perhaps the oldest and best known "school" of riding is the **Fast Ride**, an excellent form of aerobic training, and very much like a hard, fast road ride. Imagine a loop made up of some paved road, some gravel track, a stretch of single-track, and endless uphill and downhill runs. Then ride it as fast as you can. It's a competition, and all the other riders are out to beat you. The aim is the fastest loop time, so you can't afford to do anything that will slow you down. The bike is remarkably stable as you hurtle down the steep hills, and maneuverable enough to allow you to shave off vital seconds as you take each corner. Now it's another uphill run, but this Racing Bike will climb well regardless of whether you are seated or **"honking"**. There isn't much ground clearance under that big chainwheel, but the only real obstacle on this course is an old fence that you dismount for and climb over.

At the opposite end of the scale is the **Technical Trail Ride**. This time you are riding high up in the mountains. The trail is only $2\frac{1}{2}$ miles (4 kilometers) long, but it's tight, obstacle-ridden and treacherous. It's also a steep climb all the way. Riding just a short distance without stopping is a major achievement, leaving you gasping for breath and sweating profusely. Riding the trail requires the strength of a weight-lifter, the bike-handling skills of a trials rider, and the lung power of an Olympic sprinter. Flat-out attacks with nothing held back are the only

ANATOMY OF A MOUNTAIN BIKE

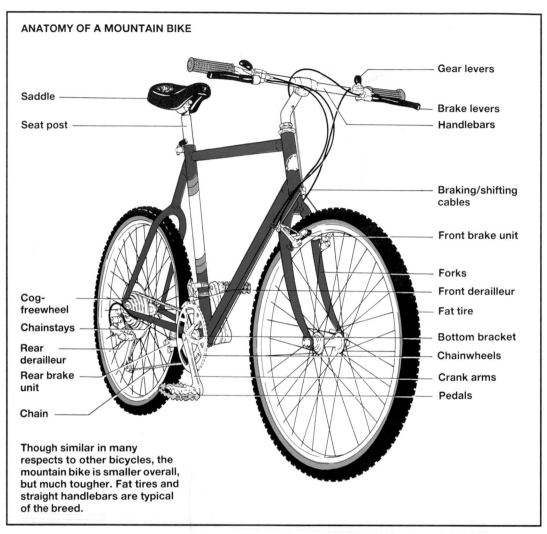

Saddle

Seat post

Cog-freewheel

Chainstays

Rear derailleur

Rear brake unit

Chain

Gear levers

Brake levers

Handlebars

Braking/shifting cables

Front brake unit

Forks

Front derailleur

Fat tire

Bottom bracket

Chainwheels

Crank arms

Pedals

Though similar in many respects to other bicycles, the mountain bike is smaller overall, but much tougher. Fat tires and straight handlebars are typical of the breed.

way to conquer the steeper segments. You rarely make it out of the lowest gear – some of your friends only HAVE one gear – and seldom get a chance to sit in the saddle. On these Technical Trail machines, ground clearance is greater than on most other mountain bikes to help avoid the many obstacles on the trail, and the top tube is low to give you some peace of mind during emergency leg-flailing. Each ride is a series of sprints up incredibly steep hills, all the time trying to ride over each obstacle in your path. The only relief comes during all-too-short recuperation periods.

For some riders, the greatest challenge is not to follow the trail all the way, but to pit their wits and their bikes against one set of obstacles for hours on end. This is the **Observed Trials** (or **Trialsin**) rider, the ultimate refinement of technical trails riding. At the very least their mounts are highly modified, but often they are built around 20-inch (51-centimeter) wheels and look nothing like a mountain bike. Purpose-built, they have one low gear, incredibly powerful brakes, and stubby little crank arms matched in size by tiny saddles which seem to be fitted more for tradition's sake than for any practical purpose.

Such machines allow the rider to perform seemingly impossible feats on incredible obstacles. Ride up a rock pile? No problem. Up that rock face? OK. Trials riders can do anything – except go anywhere!

Right: Observed Trials riding is the ultimate test for a mountain bike and its rider. The bikes are often custom-built to meet the needs and imagination of a single rider. Though they may look funny, a well-built bike and a good rider can combine to produce spectacular results.

Getting from A to B, and doing it quickly, is the goal for yet more mountain bikes. Fitted with heavy-duty street tires to allow the bike and rider to "float" over potholes and other perils in the road, these **City Bikes** serve as a tough and willing form of urban transportation. Fitted with panniers and racks, city bikes operated by courier companies can be seen weaving in and out of slow-moving or stationary traffic in many city centers. The excellent visibility afforded by the upright riding position, coupled with their wide-ranging gearing and sheer ruggedness have helped to make these machines a popular replacement for the classic 3-speed town bike.

On-road as well as off-road, the mountain bike is making its mark. City couriers like its strength and comfort, allowing them to beat bad roads and bad traffic.

MAKING THE RIGHT CHOICE

So what makes a mountain bike tick? Why is one type of bike suited to tight, mountainous, low-speed trails, while another performs best when hurtling down a steep track? And just how can a novice pick the right bike to match his or her riding style? Actually, learning to understand mountain bike design is not all that difficult, but it is important.

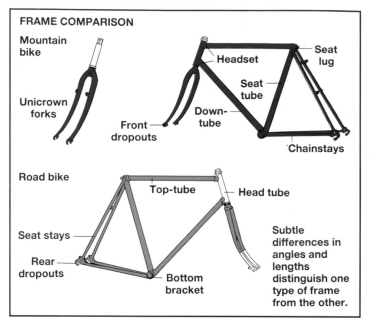

FRAME COMPARISON

Mountain bike

Unicrown forks

Front dropouts

Headset

Seat lug

Seat tube

Down-tube

Chainstays

Road bike

Top-tube

Head tube

Seat stays

Rear dropouts

Bottom bracket

Subtle differences in angles and lengths distinguish one type of frame from the other.

These are specialized machines built to withstand severe punishment time and time again, and quality does not come cheap. Anyone foolish enough to buy a bike just because it looks good is very likely making an expensive mistake.

THE FRAME

At first glance, a mountain bike frame may not look that different from any other bike, and indeed the fundamentals of the common frame pattern are very similar. But mountain bikes are a breed apart, and a closer inspection will reveal significant differences in frame geometry and construction in an attempt to achieve high standards of handling and fit. The most important dimensions of a mountain bike frame determine its handling qualities, with particular combinations of dimensions and angles producing a frame that is tuned for certain riding conditions. The key parameters are:

- Head-tube angle
- Fork offset
- Bottom bracket height
- Chainstay length
- Wheelbase

In general, stability at speed improves as you lessen the head-tube angle, lower the bottom bracket, and increase the wheelbase. Con-

DIFFERENCES IN FRAME GEOMETRY

There are several key differences in frame geometry between a mountain bike and a road bike. The former has the following characteristics:

A lower **top-tube** for better crotch clearance and saddle settings.

A higher **bottom bracket** for greater ground clearance.

A shallower **head-tube** angle for improved comfort and handling response.

Longer **chainstays** and **wheelbase** for greater stability.

A longer **top-tube** to protect the rider's knees when in the standing climbing position.

versely, agility at low speed tends to improve as you increase the head-tube angle, shorten the chainstays, and shorten the overall wheelbase. When you stand on the pedals, traction for a climb will improve significantly as the chainstays shorten, and at a lesser rate as the bottom bracket moves higher. Braking and stability on a descent will improve as the wheelbase increases, as the seat-tube angle lessens, and as the distance from the bottom bracket to the front axle increases.

So for a rider who is likely to undertake off-road riding on steep, narrow, rock-strewn footpaths, a bike that climbs well with excellent low-speed agility and good ground clearance would fit the bill, even if it does mean trading off some high-speed stability. For someone riding over wide-open, sandy plains, with mile after mile of rutted tire tracks, speed and comfort will be the foremost considerations.

FRAME DIMENSIONS AND TERRAIN

Rugged Terrain	Key Frame Dimensions
Emphasis on sufficient ground clearance; good low-speed agility; good climbing characteristics	Shorter chainstays Higher bottom bracket Steeper head-tube angle Shorter wheelbase
Smoother Terrain	Key Frame Dimensions
Emphasis on comfort and respectable speed; less importance attached to ground clearance	Longer chainstays Lower bottom bracket Shallower head-tube angle Longer wheelbase

GETTING A GOOD FIT

Just as important as the parameters which determine a mountain bike's handling qualities is the fit of the bike. In order to truly appreciate the virtues of a bike that fits you well, you have to spend some time on a bike that doesn't! Good fit is vital, and the parameters which determine how well a bike will fit your body include:

- Seat-tube angle and length
- Top-tube height and length
- Cockpit room

In the all-too-recent past, the vast majority of mountain bikes were too tall AND too short at the same time.

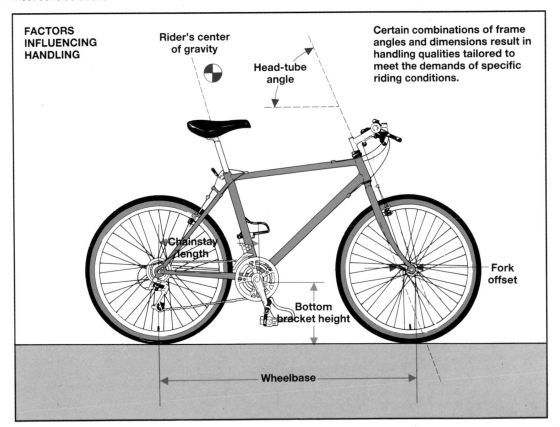

FACTORS INFLUENCING HANDLING

Rider's center of gravity

Head-tube angle

Certain combinations of frame angles and dimensions result in handling qualities tailored to meet the demands of specific riding conditions.

Chainstay length

Fork offset

Bottom bracket height

Wheelbase

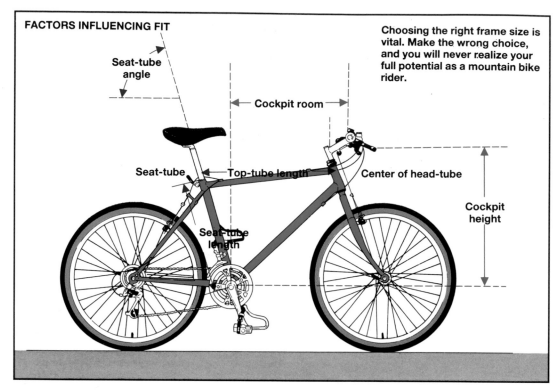

FACTORS INFLUENCING FIT

Seat-tube angle

Cockpit room

Seat-tube

Top-tube length

Center of head-tube

Seat-tube length

Cockpit height

Choosing the right frame size is vital. Make the wrong choice, and you will never realize your full potential as a mountain bike rider.

In order to get a bike with adequate cockpit room, the rider was forced to buy a tall bike with a top-tube well within "striking distance", if you know what I mean. The results could be painful to say the least! But thanks primarily to the influence of mountain bike racing, most manufacturers now produce bikes with top-tubes lengthened across the line so that a good riding position can be achieved without any real hazard.

A good fit isn't something that can be looked up in a table of figures. Many cyclists make the mistake of choosing a bike which feels comfortable to them on the dealer's floor. This is why a novice cyclist will invariably choose a bike which allows him to sit relatively upright, and that usually means handlebars which are too high, and a top-tube which is too short. This "sit up and beg" position feels fine at first, but it greatly limits power output and balance on steep hills, and so diminishes performance to a level far below the rider's potential. Many

bicycle salespersons will recommend a frame size based on standard road bike experience, with the end result being a lot of average-size riders on mountain bikes which are just too large.

When selecting a frame to fit you, stand astride the bike with your feet flat on the ground. You should allow 4 INCHES (101 MILLIMETERS) CLEARANCE BETWEEN TOP-TUBE AND CROTCH. That may sound over-generous, but the purpose is two-fold:
1. It helps minimize painful contact with the top-tube should the rider come off the saddle.
2. It allows for alterations to the position of the saddle during different types of riding.

If you already own a bike with the seat height adjusted to fit you properly, make the following calculations:
1. Measure the distance from the center of the bottom bracket axle, along the centerline of the seat tube to the top of the saddle. This distance is your **"Saddle Extension"**.

CROTCH CLEARANCE

Ground to crotch distance

Allow 4 inches (101 millimeters) clearance between crotch and top-tube for the maximum benefits when riding your mountain bike.

2. Subtract 9½ inches (24.13 centimeters) from this figure and call the result **"X"**.

YOUR OPTIMUM MOUNTAIN BIKE FRAME SHOULD MEASURE "X" FROM THE CENTER OF THE BOTTOM BRACKET AXLE TO THE TOP OF THE SEAT TUBE.

This procedure will leave you with plenty of crotch clearance and seat post for safety. In other words, you will be using the maximum practical amount of seat post. Don't make the mistake of only measuring to the intersection of the top-tube and seat tube (which is how many manufacturers list their frame sizes); measure all the way to the top of the seat tube.

Alternatively, you can find your best saddle extension by following this procedure:

1. Place your bike in a doorway or next to a wall.
2. Sit on the saddle and place your heels on the pedals.
3. Start pedaling BACKWARDS.

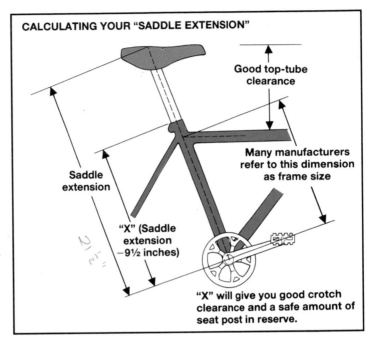

CALCULATING YOUR "SADDLE EXTENSION"

Good top-tube clearance

Many manufacturers refer to this dimension as frame size

Saddle extension

"X" (Saddle extension −9½ inches)

"X" will give you good crotch clearance and a safe amount of seat post in reserve.

CALCULATING TOP–TUBE LENGTH

"Z"

"Z" = distance from seat to base of thumb

"Z" × .48 = Optimum top-tube length

The right top-tube length will help you achieve a good riding position.

If your hips rock as you pedal, your saddle is too high. But if they don't rock, your saddle may not be high enough. If the latter occurs, raise the saddle and try again!

If you don't have a fitted bike to measure, you can approximate your saddle extension by measuring the distance from the floor to your crotch and subtracting 2 inches (5 centimeters).

You can also calculate your optimum top-tube length with this simple procedure:

1. Sit on a hard, flat surface.
2. Hold one arm straight up.
3. Measure the distance from the surface to the base of the thumb on your raised arm.
4. Multiply this figure by .48 for a reasonable approximation of the optimum length for you.

For example, my measurement from surface to base of thumb is 48 inches (122 centimeters); 48 x .48 = 23, so I should take a 23-inch (58-centimeter) top-tube. You can compensate for a short frame with a long seat stem to a limited extent, but long stems can alter the bike's handling. Always try and start with a long enough frame in the first place.

You will need to try a number of bikes for size before you make the final choice. Work with a dealership that carries a number of different brands, and ride all the different models within your price range. Take a tape-measure along and measure all the vital statistics on each bike that you ride. You will soon be able to tell how a bike will feel before you even put foot on pedal.

Left: If the frame fits, the rider can lift the wheels clear of the ground before the top-tube touches the body.

Overleaf: With the right bike and the right technique, the possibilities are endless: in this case, riding in a tin mine.

FRAME QUALITY AND CONSTRUCTION

Just as the frame geometry is important in producing a good mountain bike, so the frame construction process and the materials used help to produce bikes which can perform under the harshest of off-road conditions. Numerous materials are used in frame construction: **TIG welded titanium**; **fillet brazed chrome-moly steel**; **welded aluminum**, some **heat-treated**, some not; **cast magnesium**; TIG-welded chrome-moly and **mild steel**; **glued steel and aluminum**; **carbon and kevlar composites** . . . there may be a frame built out of pasta, for all I know.

So why is there such a choice? Consider steel: different types of steel vary greatly in the amount of stress (force per unit area) that it takes to make them fail. This level of stress is known as the material's **Yield Stress**. A mild steel, such as that used in the cheaper mountain bikes, has a yield stress of perhaps $\frac{1}{4}$ to $\frac{1}{3}$ that of a finely crafted alloy steel. However, both examples have exactly the same inherent stiffness! Take a bar of each and hang equal weights from them, and the two samples will stretch by the same amount.

You will read incessantly in the cycling press about a certain frame being stronger and stiffer and lighter, because the steel used in its tubing is of such a noble **alloy**. But the fact is that you cannot make a frame

Steel alloys are by far the most common materials used to build today's mountain bikes. Easier to work with than other metals, and very strong, steel also looks good on a high-quality bike.

Always check the quality of the joint welding on a mountain bike before you make a purchase. This lugless, brazed joint has a rough finish; a better-quality joint would be smoother.

FILLET BRAZED JOINT

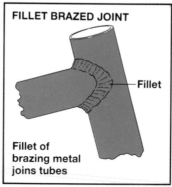

Fillet

Fillet of brazing metal joins tubes

TIG WELDED JOINT

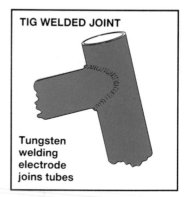

Tungsten welding electrode joins tubes

LUGGED JOINTS

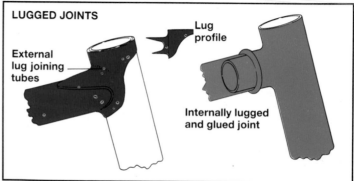

External lug joining tubes

Lug profile

Internally lugged and glued joint

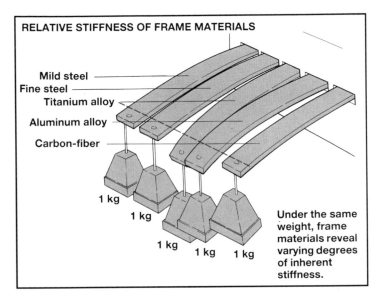

RELATIVE STIFFNESS OF FRAME MATERIALS

Mild steel
Fine steel
Titanium alloy
Aluminum alloy
Carbon-fiber

1 kg
1 kg
1 kg
1 kg
1 kg

Under the same weight, frame materials reveal varying degrees of inherent stiffness.

design stiffer just by changing the type of steel used in its construction. You can make it stronger, but not stiffer. The greater strength of the superior alloy steel would allow you to use thinner tubing, thus saving weight. Such a frame will not be as stiff as that constructed from mild steel, but it will be stronger.

The only way to make a steel frame of a given geometry both lighter AND stiffer is by increasing the outside diameter of the tubing, while making the walls of the tube thinner. Unfortunately, large-diameter, thin-walled tubes can be fragile. This fragility negates the ideal "larger diameter, thinner wall" tubing, hence the popularity of a 1.25-inch (3.2 centimeter) diameter down-tube and a 1.125-inch (2.8 centimeter) top-tube **Steel Standard**. So when you purchase a high-quality frameset, what you are getting is tubing of a standard outside diameter, but with thinner walls in proportion to the greater strength of the alloy. Your new frame will be lighter and less stiff, but probably just as strong as your old frame.

What if we build a frame of aluminum alloy? Aluminum is less dense than steel, but only $\frac{1}{3}$ as stiff. This means that an aluminum tubeset of Steel Standard diameters would have to be heavier than the steel tubing to be as stiff. However, if you

increase the aluminum's outside diameter considerably, the strength, density, diameter and wall thickness allow the construction of a frame that is lighter and stiffer than a steel frame. The aluminum is less stiff, but its lower density allows you to put it in a more effective place in the frame, resulting in greater stiffness. Unfortunately it's not always possible to use large-diameter tubing in tight areas like chainstays, between the crank and rear wheel. Several companies build half-and-half bikes, with aluminum tubing glued or bolted to steel stays for a best-of-both-worlds solution.

Titanium is no denser than aluminum, but it is $1\frac{1}{2}$ times as stiff. Compared to steel, it is half as stiff. Titanium alloys are as strong as the highest-grade steel alloys, and have the added benefit of being as corrosion-resistant as stainless steel. So why isn't titanium used more widely when it could be used to produce a frame that is potentially lighter and stiffer than both steel and aluminum frames? Apart from being horribly expensive, titanium is also difficult to machine and weld, and the price of raw tubing is not likely to come down enough in the near future to threaten steel and aluminum for the mass market frames.

An increasing number of companies are trying to design frames from the ground up to take advantage of the uniquely controllable characteristics of carbon-fiber composites. The most common approach when using these materials is to replace the steel tubes one-for-one, but the resulting frame often ends up little lighter and no stronger than the steel original. At this time, composite frames offer no overwhelming advantages over metal framesets,

---

Though metals form the basis of the vast majority of mountain bikes, composites such as carbon-fiber and kevlar are being used to a greater extent. This frame has a smoother, more rounded profile, while retaining both strength and survivability.

and, for the foreseeable future, the vast majority of mountain bike frames will be made of steel. When viewed from the standpoint of practicality, repairability, value, appearance, toughness and fatigue life, steel is the winner year after year. But rapid progress is being made, and I would venture a guess that the top-grade mountain bike frames of the future will feature composite materials to a greater extent.

COMPONENTS

Whatever its dimensions, and however it has been constructed, a frame is merely a set of tubes unless an essential range of components have been added. These are what bring the bike to life, allowing the rider to experience the thrill of mountain biking. Most of today's mountain bike manufacturers buy their components from several large Japanese companies, so the emphasis is on producing the best component quality for a given price. While it's true that you can change components more easily than you can rectify a frame with the wrong geometry, it can prove rather expensive, so again, it pays to get it right the first time.

DRIVETRAIN

If the frame is the skeleton of the mountain bike, then the drivetrain, or gear system, is its heart. Almost all mountain bikes now offer either 18- or 21-speed gearing combinations, with the ubiquitous **derailleur** system linked to a 3-**chainwheel** crank and a 6- or 7-**cog freewheel**, though in truth, nobody in their right mind would ever shift sequentially through all of the gears available on such a unit. The smallest of the chainwheels provides gears so low that they are only needed for extreme biking situations such as steep climbs, severe headwinds, and soft, clogging soils. In on-road operations, most mountain bikers would elect to start out on one of the middle chainwheel's gears, shifting up onto the largest chainwheel only when a high gear is needed, and down onto the smallest chainwheel only when heavy loads set in.

As different gears are selected via the "shifter", the chain is moved onto the relevant freewheel cog. The rider works down through the middle gears, with the rear derailleur gradually moving back to absorb looseness in the chain as it moves onto the smaller cogs.

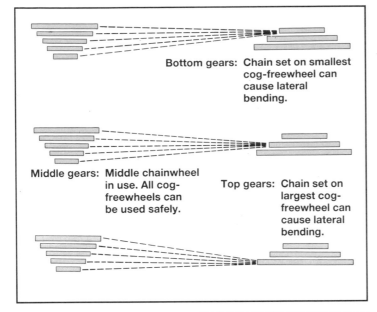

Bottom gears: Chain set on smallest cog-freewheel can cause lateral bending.

Middle gears: Middle chainwheel in use. All cog-freewheels can be used safely.

Top gears: Chain set on largest cog-freewheel can cause lateral bending.

On the majority of today's mountain bikes, the "shifters" are **"indexed"**, meaning that the right-hand lever has a definite slot for each gear setting. The old-style derailleurs, which are still available, rely on the lever being set by hand, which calls for sensitive movements.

A poorly shifting derailleur is almost always the victim either of maladjustment (including being bent by collision) or of excess shift-cable friction. As with your brakes, replace the derailleur's cables often.

Below left and below: You should be able to reach and move both "shifters" on your bike without having to take your index and middle fingers off of the brake levers, or losing your grip of the handlebars. Note how easily the thumb reaches the lever.

Some freewheel-cog combinations are best not used as they cause too much lateral bending of the chain, increasing both chain and sprocket wear. The smallest of the cogs should not be used in conjunction with the smallest chainwheel, and at the other extreme, the largest cog should not be used with the largest chainwheel. Most drivetrains will allow the middle chainwheel to be used with all of the freewheel cogs.

While it is certainly a high-maintenance item, the derailleur system is understandable, inexpensive, relatively easy to repair and simple. It is also very easy to operate, with the controls mounted on the handlebars for easy and quick use. The front derailleur (chainwheels) is controlled by the lever on the left handlebar, while that on the right controls the rear (cog-freewheels) derailleur. Both levers are connected to their respective units by **shifting cables**.

Right: "Indexed" shifters have marks to clearly identify the click-stops for each individual gear setting. Connecting cable transmits the rider's gear selection to the derailleur, which in turn moves the chain.

Friction from corroded, dirty and worn cables can destroy a bike's shifting capability, as well as robbing you of vital braking power. A bike regularly ridden in harsh conditions will need new cables as often as every 6 months. If you buy teflon-lined cables, remember that they do not need to be lubricated. And when you install your new cables, a practical touch is to solder the cut ends so that no fraying occurs. Frayed cable ends can inflict small but very painful puncture wounds if not dealt with properly.

The freewheels in the rear wheel live a difficult life. They consist of **pawls**, which allow free rotation in one direction, but lock up in the other, and many, many tiny ball bearings. Freewheels work in one of the dirtiest places on any mountain bike, but they are difficult to seal against all the muck and grime. Therefore they need replacement more often than one would like. A partially seized freewheel can have its useful life slightly extended by dribbling a little lubricant into its interior; but if a unit is suspect, the best policy is to replace it completely. A freewheel failure while you are on the move can be spectacular AND very painful!

Most bikes are fitted with three chainwheels, the front derailleur moving the chain across the teeth according to gear selection.

THE CHAIN

A gear system, whatever form its operation takes, is no good without another heavily-used item: the chain. Because they take so much punishment, chains need frequent lubrication and occasional replacement. If you ride in dirty or muddy conditions, you would be wise to lubricate your chain BEFORE EVERY RIDE. A squeeze-bottle of penetrating chain lubricant is the least wasteful (and least expensive) method of lubrication – just run the tip of the dripping bottle across each **roller** and **pin**.

A worn chain is going to eat your freewheels and cogs, creating an expensive repair bill. If your chain is bouncing off the chain-stays, or getting stuck between the tire and your U-brake located under the chain-stays, it is suffering from **"chain suck"**, a phenomenon that you can partly relieve by shortening the chain as much as safely possible.

PEDALS

Mountain bike pedals come in two main styles: those that are designed for (and need) **toe-clips**, and those that can be used with or without toe-clips. The former look like road quill pedals that have grown teeth. Viewed from above, they are short measured along the length of the bike. The latter group is squarer in outline and longer measured against the bike length.

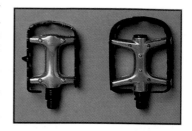

Trail pedals (right) are a good choice if you intend to undertake general riding; for serious riding, go for competition pedals (left).

The first group are **competition pedals**, and are intended for use with hard-soled (perhaps even **cleated**) mountain biking shoes, and toe-clips. If used with softer-soled running shoes, the **cages** of the competition pedals will be felt through the soles of the shoes. If used without toe-clips, the pedals will roll under your foot as you pedal, ending up under your heel. Competition pedals should only be purchased if you always intend to use toe-clips, which is not a good idea on very difficult, technical trails.

The longer pedals (I call them **trail pedals**) are slightly heavier, but are more comfortable with a greater variety of shoe types. They resist under-shoe rolling during pedaling, and are therefore favored by those who ride more difficult trails and can't use toe-clips.

If you don't yet know if you will want to ride technical trails, go for the trail pedals. They work with toe clips almost as well as do competition pedals. The latter are the current fad, but they are not as versatile.

HEADSETS

Headsets – the bearings that let the fork rotate in the frame – take a great deal of abuse in off-road riding. The lower bearing in particular is frequently smashed, so it's no surprise that headsets are a high-maintenance item. They should be adjusted whenever there is the faintest suspicion of looseness, as a loose headset will need to be replaced far sooner than will a snug-fitting one. Like all adjustable bearings, they should not be overtightened; adjust them until the slack is gone, but not so much that you feel significant resistance to rotation.

A variety of large headsets are becoming increasingly available. These distribute all of the fork-load over large bearing surfaces, increasing the life of the unit, as well as allowing a greater diameter (and therefore much stronger) fork steering tube.

TIRES AND RIMS

If there is one feature of mountain bikes that instantly distinguishes them from other types of cycles, it is the width and style of the tyres. Tyre width can be anything from $1\frac{1}{2}$ to $2\frac{1}{4}$ inches (3.8 to 5.7 centimeters), depending on what type of terrain the bike is likely to be used on. Not surprisingly, an alternative name for these machines is **"fat tire bikes"**.

Tires are components that manufacturers will frequently skimp on. There are good and bad tires, but many manufacturers assume that most people are only going to use

Riding along the cliff tops can be dangerous, but this rider has the odds in his favor thanks to good tire selection. The hard, knobby tread pattern affords excellent grip as he works his way over the rock and grass.

Contrasting tire treads, ranging from off-road knobby styles (left) to the road-only "slicks" (right).

their mountain bike for a gentle, fair-weather cruise on a Sunday afternoon. So they install narrow, **raised-rib street tires**. Such tires are absolutely worthless in the dirt. If you intend to go off-road make sure your dealer gets it right – make him fit your bike with good tires.

The type of **tread pattern** that will best suit you depends on your riding conditions. If you are likely to clock up a lot of miles on good roads, but still want to get good grip when you go off-road, a tread pattern with closely-spaced knobs will meet your needs. **Rolling resistance**

and road noise will be cut to a minimum, but they will still afford adequate grip in dry dirt. For slippery and muddy conditions, a more open tread pattern with larger gaps between the bigger knobs will be necessary. This type of tire will be slow on the road, and amuse you with a constant whine, but it will get you where you want to go in the dirt.

If you have the money for an extra set of wheels, it's wise to have a set of slick-tired wheels at hand for those road-only rides. Mounting **"slicks"** will raise your mountain bike's performance surprisingly close to that of a pure road bike.

Many mountain bike riders make the mistake of running tires with too much air pressure when riding off-road, and as a result, they suffer

from greatly reduced traction. Fact: TIRE PRESSURE IS ONE OF THE MOST IMPORTANT PARAMETERS AVAILABLE FOR ADJUSTING A BIKE'S PERFORMANCE.

If you are riding around with the manufacturer's recommended tire pressure (usually 45 PSI), you are not giving your tires a fair shake. You can gain a great deal of traction and control by letting the pressure down as low as 25 PSI. Low pressures are extremely beneficial in snow, sand, mud, or any loose soil. But too low a pressure will increase the likelihood that rocks will cause punctures by pinching your tire against the wheel rim. So if you are going to ride fast and hit rocks, increase your tire pressure. What is the correct tire pressure? That's something that can only be determined by your own experience, but if you are not getting the grip you need, try letting some air out before you invest in a set of new tires!

BRAKES

Brakes are like brains, good looks and money – you can never have too much. The brakes may feel excessively powerful in the clean, dry showroom, but they will feel all too faint the first time you point the bike down a steep, mucky descent! Since wheel rims get dirty and wet,

Fat tires sitting high off the wheel rim, and often sporting very intricate tread patterns, are a characteristic feature of virtually all mountain bikes.

only the very best brakes, working on the best rims will have enough braking power to allow safe operation on steep hills in the muck of winter.

Brakes on mountain bikes are almost always **rim brakes**, and more often than not **cantilever** or **U-brakes**, fitted with hard-wearing composite material pads. Brake pad wear should be closely monitored and the pads replaced when the grooves are nearly gone. Don't let the pads ride on the tire sidewalls – the result could be a blowout – or let them ride down, partially off the rim. Some wear coupled with a hard pull on the levers will pull the pads under the rim, and you will be left without brakes just when you really need them.

Brake levers can help or hinder your braking efforts. Short levers,

BRAKE SETTINGS

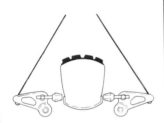

Brake blocks too high

The blocks ride on the tire sidewalls, leading to a flat tire or damaged tire casing.

BRAKE SETTINGS

Brake blocks too low

The blocks can slip under the wheel rim during hard braking, causing loss of brake power.

BRAKE SETTINGS

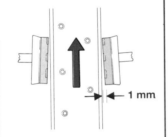

← 1 mm

The blocks should be clear of, but close to, the wheel rim.

while light and good-looking, definitely don't produce as much braking force as do full-length levers. If you ride down steep hills in wet weather, DON'T BUY SHORT LEVERS! The levers should be positioned on the handlebars so that you can use them comfortably from either the seated or standing riding positions. Most riders use their stronger index and middle fingers on the levers. If you can, you should move the levers in towards the middle of the bar so that the end of the lever is ahead of those two fingers. Pulling on the end of the lever will give you as much as twice the leverage as does pulling in the middle! Moving levers inboard, however, can cause problems with access to the thumb-shifters – so check your bike for the best position.

Above: Breakdown of Cantilever brakes (top) and U-brakes (below). Most mountain bikes are fitted with the former in both front and rear mounts; but the latter style can still be found in rear mounts, set below the chainstays and inverted to form a "U".

An example of poor brake block setting: the entire block has angled upwards, reducing the area of brake pad in contact with the wheel rim. Brake pads should make full contact with the rim.

HANDLEBARS AND STEMS

Handlebar width and stem length can be used to tune a bike to fit a given rider and operating environment. Narrow 19- to 21-inch (48- to 53-centimeter) bars work well in very tight but smooth situations, IF no obstacles are going to be crossed. If obstacles are to be attacked, a set of narrow bars will offer little leverage, resulting in poor control. Wider bars up to 24 inches (61 centimeters) produce more wind resistance at speed, but offer vastly superior bike control on sidehills, in ruts, and over obstacles. Riders with narrow bars almost always crash on the far side of logs, and are usually found riding fast on relatively smooth trails, where the reduced steering sensitivity produced by the narrow bars is an advantage.

Stem length works with a bike's top tube length and seat tube angle to determine reach and cockpit room. If your bike feels cramped, relief may be only a new stem away if your present stem is 5 inches (13.5 centimeters) long or less. A longer stem is a valuable upgrade to many older bikes, most of which were too short in the cockpit area.

To compensate for the smaller overall frame size, the mountain bike seat post is longer than that of its road bike counterpart.

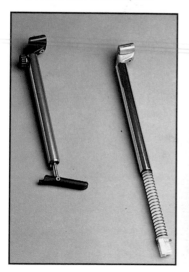

Above: Just as on road bikes, alternatives to the standard style of handlebar and rider hand positioning are becoming increasingly popular.

Above: Greater shock absorbence means greater rider comfort, hence the increasing popularity of high-tech flexistems.

Below: The longer post allows considerable extension, but with more in the seat tube for safety.

SADDLES AND SEATPOSTS

The seating apparatus on a bicycle can be the cause of great agony. A poorly-designed saddle, or one which simply doesn't conform to your anatomy, will cause you endless pain. Unfortunately, comfort in the showroom is meaningless; you cannot tell how good a saddle will feel after riding for an hour without actually riding for an hour. Wide, excessively soft saddles are very efficient at rubbing you in some awkward places, and they also prevent the rider from letting the saddle slip between his or her legs in an emergency or on severe descents.

At the other extreme, narrow, excessively firm saddles are unfortunately very good at putting all of your weight on your ischial tuberosities — the two posterior bones which you sit on. Again, the results can be most uncomfortable, and in the end, finding a saddle which is comfortable for you comes down to experimentation with different models and styles.

The seat post or seat pin is inserted into the frame's seat tube and secured with a quick-release **"binder bolt"**. There are several "adjust your saddle height on the move" devices on the market which allow the rider to loosen the seatpost quick-release, and raise or lower the saddle while in motion. All of these devices consist of a spring, adjusted to push the saddle to its road riding position, and a guide to keep the in-transit saddle pointed straight ahead. If you adjust your saddle height a lot, these devices are worth their weight in gold.

Below left and below: Raising and lowering the seat post is easy with the aid of the conveniently positioned quick-release lever.

Overleaf: With the right bike, the right components and the right skills, anything is possible.

 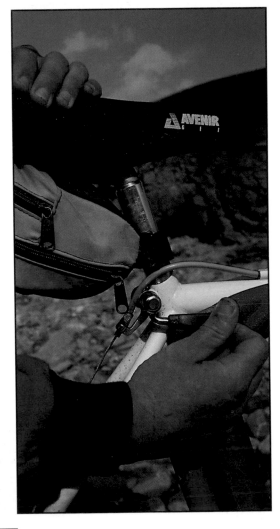

CHAPTER 2

THE HUMAN COMPONENT

Mountain biking offers a vast range of physical challenges to its practitioners. A rider can take it easy on flat roads and trails, or spend hours climbing steep mountain tracks, pushing his or her body to its limits. But regardless of which type of riding you undertake, you can be assured that you will get more from the sport by improving your fitness and strength. No matter how fit you are now, there is always room for improvement – fitness and strength are both measured on open-ended scales! This Chapter is devoted to the care and fine-tuning of the "human engine": how to protect it, how to keep it from injuring itself, and how to make it run even better. Let's start with protection.

RIDING GEAR: COMFORT AND SAFETY

The right clothes and safety items can make a good ride great, and REALLY improve a bad one. Good riding gear can make more difference to the quality of a ride than a brand new, expensive mountain bike.

A helmet is no good if it flies off when you begin to fall, so make sure you fasten the D-ring chin strap securely before a ride.

Helmets

When it comes to rider protection, the obvious place to start is also the most important: the head. Brainless riders, as a rule, perform poorly (the exceptions being found at certain downhill races); they also have no fun and little social life (except in Vancouver). To avoid joining this club, invest in a very good helmet.

Helmets are a safety item, not a fashion accessory. However, many models feature a padded interior for greater comfort.

Don't waste your money on the leather "hair nets" which are so popular among road cyclists; go for a model with a hard-shell and **nonrebounding foam** for protection. Anyone who rides anywhere without a good helmet is simply asking for trouble. I would not be around to write this book were it not for several hard helmets which gave their all on different occasions.

It may cost more, but you would be wise to invest in a hard-shell helmet (left) rather than a no-shell helmet (right). You can't put a price on protection.

If you still aren't convinced, remember that when you fall and strike your head, chances are the injury won't kill you. But you may be either brain-damaged or paralyzed to some extent. At the very least, a helmet can prevent or lessen the severe headache from a concussion resulting from one of those minor falls which are so common. And if you are wearing a good helmet when you fall, you needn't try so hard to avoid striking your head on the ground. A desperate effort to protect your head can be very costly in damage to other parts of your body sacrificed in the battle. When I fall at speed, I use my helmet, gloves and shoes as sliding points. It may sound painful, but it's a lot better than using certain other parts of the body as the points of abrasion.

Road cyclists can usually count on falling onto flat surfaces such as roads. We mountain bikers have no such luxury – when we fall, the rocks always seem to be in our landing zone. And they're sharp rocks at that. We need **penetration protection** more than road cyclists do, therefore a shell-less, foam-only helmet is of little use. It is designed to absorb energy on impact by breaking up, so it won't be around for any secondary impact. A good, tough shell coupled with non-rebounding foam provides the safest answer for a mountain biker. It will suffer compressed foam during the first impact, but it won't break up. So any secondary impact will meet at least some resistance. However, some riders are more sensitive than others to weight on their heads, and in these cases a no-shell helmet is a great deal better than no helmet at all.

One final sermon on the importance of wearing a good helmet: you don't know when "The Big One" is coming. It could be during a casual ride down an easy trail, or it could be during the last lap of a World Championship event. SO WEAR YOUR HELMET WHENEVER AND WHEREVER YOU RIDE.

Shoes

Just what type of shoe(s) will suit you best depends on the type of riding that you do. There are several important questions you should ask yourself when purchasing a pair of shoes:
● Will I be using toe-clips?
● How much tight, technical riding will I be doing?
● Is there a lot of mud in the area I ride in?
● Will I need to do a lot of scrambling on foot?

Cleated road-racing shoes or cleated mountain biking shoes are the most appropriate footwear for those who ride on paved or gravel roads all the time. If you don't intend to dismount, why not get the most efficient shoe? For those riders who need to be able to dismount quickly, most non-cleated mountain bike shoes offer a lateral ridge type of tread pattern where the sole of the shoe grips the rear pedal cage. These ridges provide a modicum of **cleat-like grip**, but mainly serve to keep the shoe from slipping on the pedal.

Below: Running shoes with a "pedal-friendly" sole (left); high-top biking shoes (middle); low-top biking shoes (rght).

Above: A solid, sturdy high-top riding shoe, held securely in place on the pedal by good sole grip and use of a toe-clip.

For all-round technical riding without toe clips, heavy, stiff-soled training-oriented running shoes with large tread blocks work very well. In this type of cycling, the rider is frequently using one foot for support or propulsion, so a shoe that can grip both the pedal (without clips) and the muddy ground is required.

Gloves

A good pair of gloves will serve several purposes for a mountain bike rider, and getting used to wearing them is a good idea. They can reduce blistering on long rides; keep your fingers warm; protect your palms if you fall; they can be less slippery on the handlebar grips than wet hands; and they can reduce arm fatigue by lowering the pressure on the **Ulnar nerve**. Fingerless bicycle gloves are good if you can find a pair with only a small amount of padding (or better, none). For arduous riding in tight terrain, motorcycle motocross-style gloves are best.

Above: Fingerless gloves allow greater dexterity, while the palm padding helps absorb much of the vibration on a hard ride.

Overleaf: This rider learnt the hard way that you can't predict an accident. Wear your safety gear!

Clothing

In most cases, I'm for it, and normal road cycling clothing usually works well. In cool weather, **lycra** or **poly-propylene** tights help keep your legs warm, but still allow free movement. Lycra tights work especially well under protective pads. DON'T WEAR JEANS! They offer neither warmth nor freedom of movement, but they will wear your skin off. Several layers of wool and/or poly-pro up top are best, and pockets in the rear of traditional bicycle jerseys are handy and practical.

A vast array of wet- or cold-weather road riding gear is available, and most of it works just as well on a mountain bike. Remember, though, that if you are riding on a difficult, steep, wooded trail on a cold day, you are going to be warmer than you think once you get your heart rate up! Wear layers, and bring along something like a **"fanny pack"** so you can store the peeled layers. Long descents can be VERY COLD, so on a cold day you should have a windbreaker and perhaps a pair of heavy gloves. On hot days, road shorts and a cotton T-shirt is a good combination. If you think you might go sliding on your favorite descent, padded mountain bike shorts are also available.

Once you have finished riding, a change of clothing is ALWAYS a good idea, especially if you are driving home. I have nearly frozen while driving home from a wet ride with the heater going full blast, simply because my cotton clothing was soaked, and I had nothing to change into.

Above: Full-length riding tights made from lycra or polypropylene are an excellent way to keep your legs warm, without restricting their movement as you pedal.

Pads

If you are the sort of rider who likes riding in very difficult terrain, then I strongly recommend you wear flexible shin and knee pads. I wear them whenever I am going on a technical ride, where I know that I will fail to make it over various difficult parts of the trail. I also wear them whenever I ride in, or practice for, trials events. With my pads in place, I know I can attack a difficult section without damaging my shins. Pads are also a blessing on those cold, wet rides as they are warm and dry.

Above: You should wear knee and shin pads as often as possible, but especially if you intend to ride on off-road trails. Once off the beaten track, obstacles are everywhere, just waiting to catch your shins and knees.

Below: When it comes to clothing for cool or cold weather rides, several thin layers are better than one thick layer as you can shed the thin layers one by one.

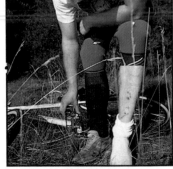

Above: If Mother Nature doesn't attack your legs, your bike probably will. Catching a shin on the teeth of an upturned pedal is extremely painful, so wear pads to avoid pedal scars.

TUNING THE HUMAN ENGINE

Stretching

All forms of cycling tend to tighten the hamstring muscles and the Achilles tendons. The hamstrings pull, ultimately, against the pelvic girdle in your lower back. When your hamstrings get too tight, you're in trouble. You are prone to tendonitis in the knees and Achilles tendons, and to inflammation in your pelvic girdle. You are also very susceptible to injury in crashes. When you crash, if you can't bend, you will break. It's as simple as that. If you don't stretch, you are increasing the likelihood of an enforced no-cycling recuperation period in the near future. Learn and use the stretching exercises illustrated – they may save you months of agony. You should spend 10 to 15 minutes warming up and stretching before and after all but the most gentle of rides. You won't, but you should.

Stretching in itself isn't enough. Many cyclists develop bad backs, not only because they don't stretch properly, but because they don't develop their abdominal muscles to match their back muscles. Strong "abs" can help hold your body up, taking much of the never-ending load off your lower back. DO YOUR SIT-UPS! At the very least, you should do 50 crunch-style sit-ups every other day.

STRETCHING EXERCISES

The Quad stretch

Keep your forward shin vertical to avoid overstretching the quadriceps in the thigh of your trailing leg.

The Hamstring stretch

Balance with hands and knee as you stretch the hamstrings at the back of the knee in your extended leg.

The lower back stretch

Gradually turn your torso in the opposite direction to that of your lower body.

The Achilles tendon stretch

Balancing with hands and right leg, try to bring the left heel to the ground to stretch the tendon.

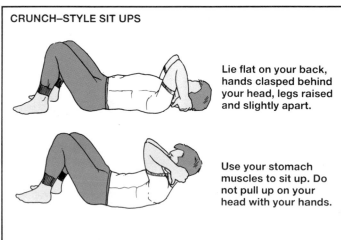

CRUNCH–STYLE SIT UPS

Lie flat on your back, hands clasped behind your head, legs raised and slightly apart.

Use your stomach muscles to sit up. Do not pull up on your head with your hands.

Aerobic fitness

If you have the time to spare, aerobic fitness is easy. All you have to do is spend 4 hours a day pedaling your bike around. Sadly, jobs, family obligations, bad weather, winter sunsets or city traffic can make cycling your way to fitness impractical. One way to beat the elements is to join a health club and participate in aerobic exercise classes, or make use of aerobic training equipment like rowing machines, stairmasters, treadmills and stationary bikes, all of which can help improve your conditioning.

My favorite winter training regimen involves a mixture of cross-country skiing, outdoor running and indoor aerobic exercise. Skiing and/

or running, while not great at developing specific pedaling muscles (that's where the rowing machine and stairmaster come in), will keep the most important part of the "engine" – the cardiovascular system – in fine tune until you take your bike out for that first ride in Spring.

Weight-lifting

Lack that extra "kick" for those really steep hills? Legs don't quite have it? Not to worry – it might not be your legs! As you will see in **Chapter 3**, your upper body muscles have a tremendous effect on your hill-climbing ability. A strong upper body can make you an almost invincible climber in those difficult situations, and the best way to develop a strong upper body quickly is to lift weights.

However, weight-lifting is dangerous, and you should not try to do it alone. The whole point of a weight-lifting program is to work each muscle group of interest to

The "Lat Pulldown" strengthens the vital Latismus Dorsi in your upper body. Make sure you don't have to overstretch to reach the bar-weight; too high a bar could lead to pulled muscles . . .

Keep your back straight and your legs crossed as you pull down on the bar-weight. Pull it down until your upper arms are parallel with the floor. Raise the bar and repeat.

The "Leg Raise" helps strengthen the Quadriceps in the upper part of your legs. Make sure you are starting with a sensible weight. Keep your back straight and your thighs flat on the bench . . .

The "Bench Press" is another exercise designed to develop upper body and arm muscles, namely your Pectorals and Triceps. Once again, choose a sensible starting weight . . .

Have a colleague close by to supervise the lifts and step in to remove the weight if you get into difficulty. Grasp the bar firmly, hands far enough apart for a balanced lift . . .

Gradually extend your arms until almost vertical. Try to keep the bar straight – don't let it move backwards over your head or you will lose control. Lower and repeat.

exhaustion, and you can't do that safely by yourself. People die trying to go for "just one more" lift. Either work out with a friend of similar strength or join a club. Like any activity, there is a good chance that you will lift the wrong way without coaching, but most clubs provide good training guidance to help you.

Both free weights and weight machines can produce good results if used intelligently and regularly. I use both and find that I can easily ride up steep slopes that I would never have dreamed of climbing before I began lifting weights, primarily due to increased upper body strength. If you can't afford to join, or don't

have access to a club, a vigorous program of dips, pull-ups, push-ups and sit-ups using only your body weight will help a lot. Remember to warm up and to stretch BEFORE AND AFTER each weight-lifting session. If you develop a sore joint, listen to your body and let it rest.

Make sure your knees are over the end of the bench, and raise the weight with your leg muscles. Bring the lower half of your legs up to the horizontal, then lower the weight and repeat.

"The Curl" helps to develop the Biceps in your upper arms. As with all weight training exercises, be sensible about the weight you intend to lift, or the results could be painful. In the start position, you should support the bar with your lower arms parallel to the ground, using the padding as support for your elbows . . .

With a firm grasp of the bar, gradually lift the weight through 90° in one smooth motion. Hold briefly in this position, then return to the horizontal with another controlled movement. In both cases, let your upper arm muscles – the Biceps – take the strain. Once back in the start position, repeat the exercise.

Moving up from the arm muscles, the "Upright Row" helps develop and strengthen the shoulder and neck muscles. Stand with your feet slightly apart, and with your hands atop the barbell . . .

With a firm grasp, lift the barbell using the shoulder and neck muscles rather than those in your arms. Keep your back straight as you bring the weight up to your midriff . . .

Then continue the upward pull, moving your elbows upwards and outwards until you reach your limit. Lower the weight to the starting position in a smooth, controlled movement and repeat.

CHAPTER 3

BASIC RIDING TECHNIQUES: LOW-SPEED SKILLS

Watching a skilled mountain bike rider work his or her way up a difficult trail or down a treacherous descent can be an awe-inspiring and bewildering experience. How can they climb such steep hills? How do they get their bikes over those obstacles? And how can they come down that slope with such control when most people couldn't manage it on foot? Just as impressive is watching a skilled racer making a smooth and controlled high-speed descent on a steep trail or dirt road; or pounding up a seemingly infinite grade in middle gear. Just how do they do it?

A mountain bike rider's abilities are based on the following:

1. Aerobic fitness
2. Anaerobic strength
3. Bike-handling skills

While achieving high levels of fitness and strength is fairly straightforward for a healthy rider (a lot of riding and exercise), mastering the riding techniques needed for off-road mountain biking can take years without coaching. Fortunately, there are a few basic principles which, if learned well, will soon have you impressing other riders. This Chapter is devoted to those principles; the basics of riding a mountain bike on level terrain, downhill, uphill and over small obstacles. A few simple skills in each area will be enough to get you out into the woods and up

into the hills with a sound foundation on which to build through experience. And if you take the time to work on the associated exercises, these principles will also reduce your chances of injury or, even worse, humiliation during your initiation period.

Right: Successful low-speed balancing depends on a rider's ability to judge the moment at which the bike loses stability.

Below: If you can master the art of low-speed riding, you are on the way to being able to take on very tricky obstacles.

LOW-SPEED BALANCE: HOW TO SURVIVE RIDING OUT OF THE PARKING LOT

Bikes have a certain speed range in which they actually help the rider's balance. Within this range, hands-off riding is possible, and riding in a straight line is easy. Below a certain speed, the bike does little to help and, in fact, demands the rider's full attention. Learning to balance well in this difficult low-speed regime is vital if you hope to take your mountain bike off-road, since you will be faced with numerous situations where anything other than low speed will be impossible. This is true

even if your only goal is to race, as most courses include several tricky sections which offer you the choice of dismounting and pushing, or slowing down and riding through in style and control. Learning low-speed balance techniques will help you no matter what type of riding you have your heart set on.

STANDING RIDING

Most of the more advanced low-speed riding skills that you will learn in this book require you to stand up, as sitting in the saddle greatly reduces the low-speed maneuverability and balance potential of the bike. You, the rider will also suffer if

you can't stand up as your body motion will be very limited – you can't exert the body in ways needed to perform certain maneuvers, or stay in control in difficult situations if you can't move freely. And a body stuck to a saddle cannot move freely. Finally, the presence of upwards of 90 pounds (41 kilograms) on the saddle means that when the back wheel hits a bump, it must lift most of that weight. It might just as well stop rolling. instead, and it often does.

But a standing rider can easily ride over a slippery tree root, for instance, without touching it with either wheel. And you can't slip on an obstacle that you don't touch. Fast descents are best done with only very light pressure on a slightly lowered saddle. Again, you must get used to the feeling of stand-up riding. However, it can be very tiring, since your legs must not only propel you but also support your body weight. So if you are concerned about saving energy, you should only use the standing riding position when you really need it.

Learning the technique is straightforward. Take your bike to an open field or park, or some other wide-open, safe, car-free area. Lower your saddle as far as it will go to remove any temptation to sit down, and set your bike in a low gear (26–30 gear-inches). With the first and second fingers of both hands resting lightly on your brake levers, push off and start pedalling. If you start with your left foot on the ground, your right pedal should be at the 2 o'clock position as you start out, so that you will get the maximum time from that single power stroke in which to place your left foot properly on the pedal.

You will find that balancing at low speed is easier if you drag both brakes slightly, so that you have some resistance to work against. Your arms should be fairly relaxed, allowing the bike to steer itself. YOU DON'T STEER BY PUSHING AND

Above left and left: For the standing riding start, your foot should be in the 2 o'clock position. As you push off, bring the other foot through.

Correct positioning of index and middle fingers for effective brake dragging, enabling you to cancel out any surplus pedal power before you lose control.

• Your bottom should not be sticking out.
■ In short, you should look a bit like someone with their hands on a table, about to spring off in a new direction. You need to have some travel left in your limbs in both directions (compression and extension) in case your bike moves in an unanticipated direction. If you were standing ramrod straight, and the bike darted to one side, you would be left behind.

Turning corners
When you feel comfortable with the straight-line exercise, it's on to **Turning At Low Speeds While Standing**. Again, you should have your fingers ready on the brake levers, ready to drag the brakes to smooth out your power flow. When you turn to the left, which way

• Divide your body weight between your arms and legs.
• Stand in a natural, springy position with your back in a relaxed half-slump.

Good use of the body for low-speed cornering: nose above the outside grip; outside elbow bent.

PULLING ON THE HANDLEBARS; YOU STEER BY MOVING YOUR SHOULDERS AND HEAD FROM SIDE TO SIDE, LETTING YOUR BIKE REACT TO THE CHANGE IN YOUR BALANCE POINT BY STEERING ITSELF. Forcing the bike to turn by **"sawing"** at the bars at low speed tends to set up an oscillatory steering instability, and you'll soon be weaving about like a drunken sailor. Your arms should take some of your body's weight, but they should also allow the handlebars to turn relatively freely.

EXERCISE No. 1
Try to ride along a straight feature on the ground. See just how slowly you can ride without losing your ability to follow the line. Remember:
• Keep your arms relaxed; don't let them fight the bicycle.
• Balance by shifting your upper torso back and forth in small, smooth motions.
• Focus your eyes 3 to 10 feet (0.9 to 3 meters) ahead of your front wheel, with occasional glances ahead to ensure you don't run into something.

should you shift your torso? Most people shift their shoulders into the corner and back. This is precisely the wrong response!

There are two factors at work here:

1. Tires grip best when they have weight on them. So you want to shift a bit of your weight onto the hard-working front tire by leaning slightly FORWARD when you are turning.

2. The geometry of a bike causes the front wheel to turn in the direction that the frame leans.

At low speed, your body's center of gravity must stay in a near vertical plane above the tires' contact point, unless you are falling over. If you lean your body into a turn, the bike has to lean out of the turn to maintain your equilibrium! Thus, the front wheel wants to steer OUT of the turn. If, on the other hand, you shifted your torso out of the turn, the bike would lean INTO the turn, and the front wheel would be happy to oblige your turning request of its own free will.

To sum up: if you are turning to the RIGHT, your nose should move out to the LEFT and FORWARD, approaching the space above your LEFT handgrip.

Left: Starting into the turn, the rider stays upright but with his body weight shifted slightly forward. This movement of weight presses down on the front wheel for better grip.

Above: Though he is turning to the left, the rider's body is leaning the opposite way to maintain the bike's equilibrium. Note how his nose is aligned with the outside handlebar.

Hard surfaces

Turning at low speed on a hard surface can be very difficult if you don't drag your brakes lightly, because powerful legs in a low gear feel almost no resistance. With no resistance, you will speed up every time a leg goes through a **power stroke**. Speed in a corner is an important factor in determining the course you must follow to keep from falling over, and erratic speed changes resulting from power surges makes balancing and line-keeping difficult. Balancing is much easier in a corner if you pedal against light resistance from your brakes, thus stabilizing your speed. Try it!

EXERCISE No. 2

This will help improve your low-speed turning capability. Set up a figure-of-eight course with two turns of 6½ to 13 feet (2 to 4 meters) radius. Mark the inside and outside of the course with stones, sticks or whatever is at hand. Now ride around the course as slowly as you can while standing. Remember:
● Get that nose out over the outside handgrip.
● Don't forget to drag your brakes lightly.
● Start at a moderate speed.

Try a competition with yourself, or with your friends, to see how slowly you can negotiate the course without "**dabbing**". When you are confident, tighten the course up; and when this gets to be old hat, reposition the course on a slight grade. Now brake-dragging becomes really important! You will want to maintain the same speed uphill and down, and you can only do so with a smooth transmission from power to braking at the top, and from braking to power at the bottom of the curve. The best answer is to always pedal and always drag your brakes, changing the relative strength of each depending on whether you are climbing or descending. A smooth transition from climbing to descending is easier if both pedaling and braking are continuous.

A tight corner on a hard surface: two good reasons to cover the brake levers.

When you have mastered standing riding in straight lines and corners, you have taken a significant step towards the off-road mastery of your bike. Remember, for low speed, standing riding:
● Stand in a natural, relaxed position.
● Don't let your arms tense up.

● Lean OUT of a turn and FORWARD.
● Drag your brakes in low-speed corners for stability.
● Steer by shifting your body weight, not by "sawing" at the bars.
● Develop the ability to ride in the straight line OF YOUR CHOICE.
● Finally, RELAX!

BRAKING: LEARNING TO LOVE THE FRONT BRAKE

Which brake should you use when you are descending an imposing slope? The correct answer is BOTH, but a disturbing number of people would choose the rear brake exclusively. While it is true that a grossly misused front brake can, under certain circumstances, bring the back wheel up and unceremoniously dump the rider over the 'bars, it is also true that lack of skill in the use of the front brake due to a fear of flipping over is probably the most dangerous flaw a rider can have.

Why? Because the front brake offers the vast majority of a bicycle's potential stopping power. The harder you stop, or the steeper the hill you descend, the greater the transfer of braking potential to the front wheel. The corollary is also true: when you stop quickly or use the brakes while on a steep descent, the back wheel is either very light or not touching at all. A rider relying on the rear brake exclusively has a severely limited stopping capability. Just as serious,

Descending a hill under control is impossible unless you know how to position your body, and use the front brake correctly.

use of the rear brake only puts a severe limit on the slope that can be descended in safety.

LEARN TO LOVE THE FRONT BRAKE. IT IS YOUR BEST FRIEND!

Grip

How much grip can a tire produce? The answer depends on:
● Tire tread.
● Rubber compound.
● The nature of the riding surface.
● The force pushing the tire into the ground.

When you brake, you slow down. As you decelerate, your body's center of gravity wants to keep going. As long as you are decelerating, weight is being transferred from the back wheel to the front wheel. If you brake very hard, all of the weight that was holding the rear wheel down will be transferred to the front wheel, and the rear wheel will rise into the air with any further braking effort. As weight moves from the back wheel, the amount of braking force it can transmit to the ground without locking up and sliding decreases proportionally. No weight on the back wheel means no braking force from the back wheel.

Another bothersome property of tires is that during braking, cornering or acceleration, they produce the most grip just before they lock up. As they lock up and slide over

the ground, the braking or cornering or driving force that they produce falls off sharply. Not only does a sliding wheel offer little stopping power, it's also just as happy to slide sideways as forward while offering little directional stability.

Get the idea? THE BRAKING POWER OF THE REAR TIRE IS STRICTLY LIMITED. Because weight transfers off of the rear tire when a bike stops or descends, the amount of brake that can be applied before the rear wheel slides is limited; and when the rear wheel slides, its braking force is reduced still further.

The front brake, on the other hand, just gets more potent the harder you decelerate. The harder you stop, the more weight is transferred onto the front wheel; and the more weight transferred onto the front wheel, the more braking force you can transmit, and the harder you can stop – at least until you flip over the 'bars. You can control the tendency to flip by either altering the pressure on the front brake lever, moving your body rearward on the bike, or both.

EXERCISE No. 3

Here are some simple exercises to teach you how to use your brakes properly. The lessons you will learn will be equally applicable to crawling down a steep descent deep in the woods, or to flying into a tight corner on a race course.

Find a wide, open, smooth-surfaced dirt slope of moderate steepness, with a good runout at the bottom. The slope should not be a tall one, so that nothing serious will happen to you if you panic and scream down the hill completely out of control. At the very least, wear your helmet and gloves. Pads are also recommended, and, as always, you should stretch before you ride. You should try these exercises in both the sitting and standing riding positions, since you will be stopping and descending both ways in real life. Most riders set up their bike with the front brake controlled by the left lever, and the rear unit controlled by the right lever. Check your bike before you try these exercises – you MUST know which lever controls which brake.

Above: This rider is about to put all of his faith in the front brake with spectacular results . . .

Below: With no rear brake power, and full force on the front unit, the rear wheel rises further . . .

Above: His body weight is too far forward, so as he begins to brake, the rear wheel rises . . .

Below: The situation is out of control, and the rider is thrown over the handlebars.

Here are some tips for a safe descent:

1. Start down the hill at the speed that you want to maintain; don't try to decelerate on the hill.

2. Try to minimize the skidding of the back wheel by using as much front brake as you can without lifting the back wheel.

3. Keep the rear wheel rolling.

4. Use the two inside fingers on each hand for braking, leaving the outer pairs of fingers around the grips for control. THE FINGERS ON THE BRAKES MUST BE FLEXIBLE, NOT FROZEN.

5. If the hill is steep, lower your saddle BEFORE you commit yourself to the descent.

6. NEVER, EVER take both feet off of the pedals on a descent. One foot off is the absolute limit. If you do take both feet off, you will inevitably slide forward on the bike, flip, and land on your face.

The correct way to descend: body pushed back and downward.

front wheel with too much brake, the wheel probably won't slide; it's likely to have enough braking traction to lift the back wheel (and the rider) off the ground. Don't panic if this happens; release the pressure on the front brake lever slightly, and the back wheel will come right back down.

Have you got that mastered? Are you bored with slow descents straight down the hill? We'll soon fix that. Set up an S-turn down the hill. Try to ride down the course without touching foot to ground, slowly and in control. You will find that you don't need to lean forward much, since so much of your weight is on the front wheel already, but you will need some sensitive fingers on the brake levers! Try to turn the corners like a snake, with no quick movements. Everything should be done smoothly.

it than fitness. You must learn to read the terrain; to use momentum; to steer at low speeds on steep hills; and to shift positions to save your muscles. On steeper or more technical hills, you will have to stand up again, I'm afraid! But since seated climbing will be more common, we will start there.

Above: Taking both feet off of the pedals while descending is a sure way to injure yourself.

With these tips in mind, try to ride down the hill as slowly as possible without locking up either wheel. You will find that with equal pressure on the front and rear brake levers, the rear wheel will lock up and slide first. When you detect that a wheel is sliding, ease back the pressure on that lever slightly. You must play with **"lock-up"** to learn when it occurs and what it feels like. Try to lock up the rear wheel, releasing the pressure immediately after lock-up so that the wheel rolls again before you lose balance. If you lock up the

HILLCLIMBING

Climbing hills on a mountain bike can be very easy. After all, these bikes have very low gearing and fat, knobby. tires for just this reason. The unknown factor on many a hill-climb is rider fitness. Can you produce the power to maintain steerage way, and have enough momentum to carry you over the odd loose or slippery area on the trail? It turns out that there is more to

Above: Using good technique is just as important when it comes to riding uphill. This rider is using the jockey position to boost rear wheel traction.

Right: To ride successfully over soft surfaces like gravel, sand and snow requires a constant application of power and not too much weight on the front wheel.

Your saddle should be adjusted to precisely the right height for seated climbing. An inch too low, and your legs will tire rapidly. An inch too high, and you can damage your Achilles tendons. A bike with too short a reach from the saddle to the handlebars can also hinder your climbing performance.

Beginners frequently fail in hill-climbing attempts, not because they run out of grip or power, but because they can't steer a good line up the hill. A climbing cycle is a very sensitive device; it is all too easy to get it off course and wobbling with ham-fisted steering corrections. What should you do? Forget steering with your hands! Steer by shifting your weight. Let the bike do the steering – you just keep out of its way. Do NOT steer by turning the bars back and forth; to do so means starting the dreaded climbing wobble. Look ahead, relax, and will the bike to go where you are looking. Your body and the bike will take care of the details.

There are usually a number of paths or lines up any given hill. A good climber will read the hill, looking for the path of least resistance and most plentiful traction. Small piles of loose gravel, for instance, can lead to **wheelspin**, and that means a loss of forward motion and failure. Relatively small increases in local slope can spell disaster – the difference in slope between a difficult climb and an impossible climb can sometimes be very small. Good riders know how to find moister soil, or how to use large, imbedded rocks to their advantage. Reading the terrain is an absolutely vital skill for any mountain biker, and this is particularly true on a hillclimb.

Mountain bikers are frequently forced to ride through patches of loose gravel, sand, mud or other traction-robbing detritus on a hillclimb. The key to survival lies in the proper use of anticipation and momentum. If you can gather some extra energy for a mini-sprint just before the offending patch, the extra speed will often carry you through successfully. Just before the loose patch, accelerate from your uphill cruising speed. As your back tire touches the slippery patch, you reduce your power as much as you can get away with. As soon as the back tire is back on a good surface, turn on the power again. Obviously these mini-sprints are tiring, so avoidance is often better.

STANDING UP TO IT ALL

Many novice riders know only one way to climb a hill: they will sit in one position on the bike, using one set of muscles until they are glowing with heat. A knowledgeable rider will shift around on the saddle and stand up occasionally, thus shifting the strain from one set of muscles to another.

When should a rider stand up? When he or she needs to. Standing when climbing is required not only as a way to relieve your tired, sit-down pedaling muscle groups, but also as a way to surmount the most difficult of climbs.

When a rider stands up to pedal up a hill, it is natural to end up in a road rider's climbing position. Roads offer good traction, in general, so road riders don't need to be so careful in maintaining the rear tire's share of the weight. They can let their buttocks come forward to-wards their handlebar stems, with no slippage of the rear tire. But if you do this in a typical off-road climbing situation, there will not be enough weight on the rear tire to let it get the grip it needs, so it will spin easily. Two related techniques will alleviate this problem:

1. A new riding position for climbing.
2. A very powerful dynamic traction technique that can also help the seated rider.

THE JOCKEY POSITION: THE KEY TO SUCCESSFUL STANDING CLIMBING

Sir Isaac Newton showed the world that force is required to accelerate a mass. A gravitational field (like the one surrounding the earth) is an acceleration: you would accelerate towards the center of the planet if you weren't supported by terra (usually) firma. When you climb a hill

Good standing climbing position: the rider's forehead is brought down over the handlebars; this forces more of his static weight back over the rear wheel.

Using your Static Weight Balance to increase climbing grip is fine, but you have only so much weight. As the hill steepens or surface conditions worsen, you need more and more traction, and thus more and more weight on your rear wheel. You can take only so much weight from your front wheel before you either fall over backwards, or lose it because of a lack of steering control. Fortunately, there is a very powerful method that can apply more vertical force to the rear tire than your total weight could account for. To do this, we add another source of acceleration.

While in the jockey position on a hill, if you pull the handlebars back towards your chest sharply and quickly, you will be trying to accelerate your chest towards the handlebars. Your body does accelerate towards the bars, but the bars also accelerate back and up towards your chest. The bike frame tries to rear up, but is met by resistance

on your mountain bike, the ground is reacting to the forces generated by your combined bike-and-rider mass being acted upon by gravity. If you move that combined center of gravity, which is somewhere forward of your hip bones, to the extreme rear of the bike, your rear wheel will take all of the load. If you shift your *cg* far forward, the front wheel will take more of the load. The proportion of gravitational force taken by each wheel is called the **Static Weight Balance**.

The jockey position puts your body into a shape such that slightly more of the static weight is carried by the rear wheel, thus increasing traction. What's more, the jockey position makes it easy to make all of the fine positional adjustments you will perform when climbing.

Getting into the jockey position is easy:
1. Stand up, but bring your forehead down towards your stem. This forces your rear end back.
2. Let your elbows swing outboard a little.

You are now in the jockey position: a low, compact position that will let you climb powerfully. The jockey position increases the static load on the rear tire, but leaves some load on the front tire for steering.

Bad standing climbing position: the rider's hips are too far forward, severely reducing the rear wheel traction. In just a short time, this rider will be completely exhausted.

DYNAMIC TRACTION

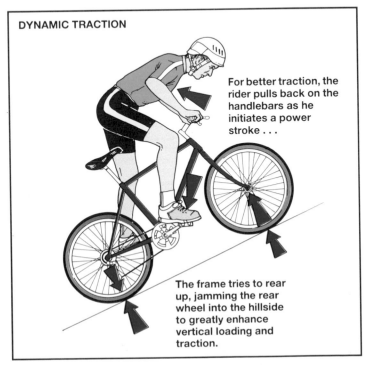

For better traction, the rider pulls back on the handlebars as he initiates a power stroke . . .

The frame tries to rear up, jamming the rear wheel into the hillside to greatly enhance vertical loading and traction.

when it tries to accelerate your body vertically at the pedals. Since it can't move your feet as much as it would like to, the bike frame has to press down on the rear tire to compensate. The bike becomes a lever, and your body mass becomes the fulcrum. The amount of vertical force that you can add to the static rear wheel load in this fashion is amazing. You can easily double the amount of vertical load (and potential traction) with the dynamic loading method.

Unfortunately, this doubling lasts only as long as the acceleration lasts – a fraction of a second. The potential for increased traction can only be of use if the dynamic pulse happens to come during a power stroke! It all works out right after some practice if you follow this procedure:

1. When your right leg is just entering its powerful down-stroke, pull back mainly with your right arm by tightening your right **latismus dorsi** ("lat") muscle. The pulse of traction comes at the same time as the pulse of driving force and you squirt ahead with the enhanced grip.

2. When your left leg reaches its power stroke, your left "lat" tightens up quickly, and away you go.

During each pulse, your front wheel may come off the ground, but since your static weight balance has left some weight on the front end, it will come back down as soon as the pulse is complete. You can steer in the interval between pulses. You can also use the light front end as a balancing and steering aid, placing the front end to either side as appropriate for balance or course correction.

This technique is extremely potent. If you master it, you will be able to get traction on extremely steep, slippery slopes. You will be limited only by your own strength. This method requires a good amount of upper body strength, and also a good sense of rhythm and timing. If your timing is off, the technique will just be a waste of energy.

Speaking of energy, the dynamic loading technique burns energy at a profligate rate. Think of it as an afterburner – you can't leave it in all of the time, but it's there when you need it.

CROSSING OBSTACLES

The best riders can ride mountain bikes over amazingly large obstacles. There is a rider in Portland, Oregon who has cleared a 46-inch (117-centimeter) log without touching it – and he rode away after landing. Now, you may not be interested in riding over such logs, but you should be interested in learning how to ride over smaller obstacles. All interesting trails offer small obstacles, and bad technique can turn such impediments into hazards.

THE WHEELIE – LOFTY THOUGHTS FOR THE FRONT WHEEL

The basic idea is that you don't want to ram either wheel into an obstacle. You want to "float" both wheels over the obstacle, or at least get out of the bike's way so that it can deal with the impediment.

Start on a level, hard surface with nothing to hit. As always, don your protective gear – it's easy to fall over when you are learning something new. To prepare for lofting the front wheel, slowly ease your torso forward as if you were looking at your front tire. Now accelerate your upper body backwards, stopping it suddenly by stiffening your arms. The inertia of your body will bring the front wheel up a bit, or at least lighten it. If you combine this sudden rise with a simultaneous power stroke from either leg, your wheel will come up higher. Again, give your body some rearward and upward velocity, then snub it by pulling on the bars. At the precise instant of the pull, give a power stroke – and that's a wheelie.

Below: To perform a successful wheelie, move your body well forward; then pull back to lift the front wheel . . .

Above: A combination of body inertia and a strong power stroke will lift the wheel onto the log.

Wheelies can also be done at speed, but since you will be in a much higher gear, you won't get much help from the power pulse. A high-speed wheelie is done purely with body inertia.

Wheelies should ultimately be executed with timing rather than brute, bar-bending force. Keep working on them until you can loft your front wheel over some mark on the ground reliably. When you are confident of your ability, it's on to . . . an obstacle! Find an obstacle of modest height like a curb. You should check that your chainwheels cannot hit the obstacle. If they do, find a lower obstacle.

When you are ready, follow this procedure:

1. Ride up to the curb at slow but not dead slow speed.

2. Execute a wheelie at precisely the right time (when your front wheel is roughly 7.8 inches [20 centimeters] from the curb).

3. Land your front wheel atop the curb.

Don't worry what the rear wheel does; ignore it for now. Keep practicing until your timing is accurate and you have a good feeling for what your body needs to do.

Now let's work on the back wheel. When you learn to ski, you are taught to "unweight" just before initiating a turn. This is done to remove the static weight from the skis so that they will be easily turned. The same thing applies here:

● Unweight the rear wheel AFTER the front wheel has landed, just an instant before the rear wheel gets to the curb.

● Unweight by leaning forward, towards the bars.

● Stop your lean by stiffening your arms.

THE WHEELIE

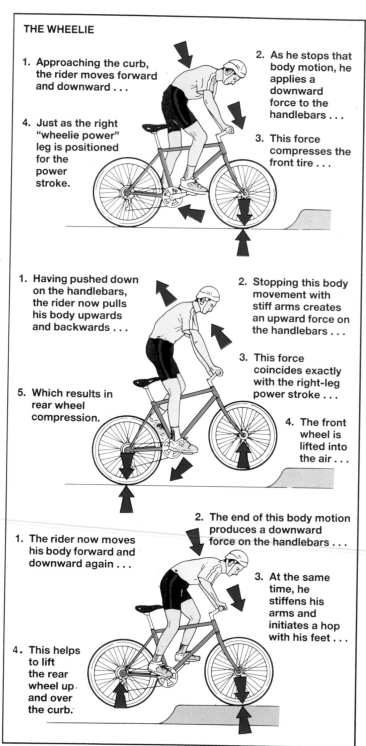

1. Approaching the curb, the rider moves forward and downward . . .

2. As he stops that body motion, he applies a downward force to the handlebars . . .

3. This force compresses the front tire . . .

4. Just as the right "wheelie power" leg is positioned for the power stroke.

1. Having pushed down on the handlebars, the rider now pulls his body upwards and backwards . . .

2. Stopping this body movement with stiff arms creates an upward force on the handlebars . . .

3. This force coincides exactly with the right-leg power stroke . . .

4. The front wheel is lifted into the air . . .

5. Which results in rear wheel compression.

1. The rider now moves his body forward and downward again . . .

2. The end of this body motion produces a downward force on the handlebars . . .

3. At the same time, he stiffens his arms and initiates a hop with his feet . . .

4. This helps to lift the rear wheel up and over the curb.

Just as your arms stiffen, give a little hop with the balls of your feet.

The rear wheel goes into the air, sailing up and over the curb. The sequence for the entire curb-crossing is:
- Approach.
- Lean back.
- The wheelie.
- Lean forward.
- Unweighting of the rear wheel.
- Return to center, and pedal off into the sunset.

Once you can ascend the curb without touching it, you will be able to use the same technique on trails in slippery root-avoidance, for instance. As the obstacles get bigger, the wheelie and rear wheel-hop have to increase apace in height. This technique can grow to handle obstacles of up to 3 feet 3 inches (1 meter) in height – you simply do a higher wheelie and hop harder.

Conventional general-purpose mountain bikes have a problem with obstacle crossing: ground clearance. Most riders don't need to cross obstacles that are so large that their chainwheels will strike. If you find that you are frequently hitting your chainwheels on obstacles on your favorite rides, you have a difficult choice to make. You can:
- Ignore the problem, and keep on replacing chainwheels.
- Remove the largest diameter chainwheel, thus slightly increasing the ground clearance.
- Stop every time you come to a serious obstacle.
- Buy a bike with a higher bottom bracket.
- Simply not ride where there are larger obstacles.

Or you could learn to hop your rear wheel onto the log just after the front wheel gets there, so that the chainwheel sails right over the obstacle with room to spare. This technique requires a powerful hop with some forward propulsion in it. Try it on your curb! Give yourself a bit of forward thrust with a push on the pedal just as you hop.

LOOSE SURFACES

When the surface gets loose, loosen up yourself. Soft, power-sucking soils; pea-gravel; beach rocks; snow . . . all are very difficult to ride in. Simply maintaining forward motion is a challenge, never mind turning or climbing.

The key to these surfaces is to keep the power on, and the weight back. Skim the front wheel over the surface so that it can't dig in. DRIVE with the back wheel. If you are going from a good surface to a loose one, slow down before getting to the soft stuff, then accelerate into it with your static weight biased strongly towards the rear wheel. Now keep the power on and, no matter what happens, don't steer by turning the bars. To steer means to dig the front wheel into the surface, and you know what that means: launch time.

An effective wheelie relies on good balance and weight shift.

CHAPTER 4

ADVANCED RIDING TECHNIQUES: LOW SPEED

While most of the riding techniques described in this Chapter are derived from Observed Trials competition, you can still benefit from the information without competing in such events. Though they are difficult and require some practice, mastering advanced low-speed techniques will make your trail riding a lot more fun. You may be primarily interested in fast riding, but many fast trails have difficult technical sections. Wouldn't you rather have the skills to get you through these awkward parts of a trail? Superior bike-handling skills will help you, no matter what your riding style, and the techniques

covered here will hone your riding sharpness to a fine edge.

All of these maneuvers require a lot of freedom of movement as you will be standing up and moving your body around more than in any other kind of mountain bike riding. This means that your saddle will have to be lowered as far as possible for comfort and safety. It also means that you will be in trouble if you are riding a large bike with a top-tube that is too high, so your bike MUST be set up properly (see **Chapter 1** on choosing the right frame).

Finally, learning these riding techniques is brutal on both bike and rider, so you would be well advised

to wear ALL of your protective gear, including knee and shin pads.

VERY STEEP CLIMBS

A very common obstacle in mountain biking is the steep climb. Often short, they are hard enough for hikers, let alone mountain bikers; but a skilled rider can climb such slopes, even if it is only for limited distances. The

Out of the saddle and pedaling hard, this rider illustrates the right way to combine upper body strength with leg power to get the most out of each power pulse.

exertion required from every muscle in your body during an attack on such a slope is so great that your maximum endurance will be measured in a matter of seconds.

However, there are some basic tips that will make such climbs slightly easier:

• Stand up, get into the jockey position, and use dynamic rear wheel loading (see **Chapter 3**).

• Approach a steep slope in the proper gear (around 26 **gear-inches**).

• Don't hit the hill with maximum speed – hit it with maximum acceleration.

• Your maximum pedal effort should occur as your rear wheel hits the slope. At this point, the hill is forcing your body mass to change direction, and the rear tire feels this as an increased downforce.

• Use your upper body strength to climb the hill; you will be climbing the hill as much with your latismus dorsi as your legs. Your initial momentum up the hill will soon die away, so you must use **dynamic rear wheel weighting** very strongly to get the traction and propulsion you need to keep moving. Most steep slopes have a very narrow line, and your bike will try to fall off of that line, so steering is vital. DO NOT STEER BY TURNING THE HANDLEBARS! Each time you perform a **dynamic weight transfer contraction**, say with your right side, your bike will swing to the left with the front wheel slightly off the ground. Let the front wheel move off to the left just as you force your left-side muscles to pump out another **power pulse**.

Left: On steep, narrow climbs, good upper body strength is vital if you are to succeed. Don't rely solely on your legs.

Overleaf: In complete contrast to steep ascents, steep descents offer another set of challenges to the mountain bike rider.

Descending on a mountain bike can be a dangerous business if you don't follow certain rules. The key to success is keeping your speed under control, so learn to drag your brakes.

This will swing the front wheel around to the right. Your course up the hill is the average of these two directions, and the front wheel stays pointed straight ahead, relative to the bike. The **twice-per-crank-revolution** touches of the front wheel will allow you to choose your path up the slope.

VERY STEEP DESCENTS

What goes up must come back down, and steep descents are just as common on any given trail as are steep climbs. Many riders fear steep descents, and for good reason – when coming down a steep slope, a rider is always close to an unscheduled flight over the handlebars. An unanticipated soft-spot can easily trap the front wheel, throwing you

onto your face; an unseen depression on the flat **runout** can stop your front wheel, again with dire consequences; and you can show poor judgement when using the front brake, or in positioning your body for the ride downhill. On the other hand, once you learn the correct braking and body positioning skills to handle steep descents, **dropoffs** become a thrill.

Short Dropoffs
When preparing to descend a short, steep dropoff, you should follow these tips:

1. As you approach the dropoff, get off your bike and approach the edge on foot. Survey both the slope and the landing site before you start your descent, making sure that there are no wheel traps. If there are, think about what you will have to do to avoid them.

2. Return to your bike and make sure that your saddle is set as low as possible. If it is too high, you will soon feel the Hand of Mother Nature pushing you over the handlebars!

3. Drag your brakes as you approach the edge, both to bring your speed under control, and to make sure that your fingers know where the brake levers are.

4. Ride up to the drop in your normal standing position.

5. As you approach the edge of a sharp dropoff, you won't be able to see the surface of the slope itself. You must aim for some previously chosen feature on the edge in order to align yourself with your desired line.

Right: As he goes over the edge of this very steep descent, the rider pushes the handlebars well away and stays out of the saddle.

Below: Good use of the steep descent position. Rear wheel weighting is enhanced by the rider's body position.

6. Move into the steep descent position: as the bike rolls over the edge, push the handlebars away from you. Let the bike roll forward while you position your upper body well back, so that when you are on the slope, you are in the proper position. Don't move your body back until you are actually going over the edge.

7. If you roll over the edge of the hill too tentatively, your front wheel will try to fall sideways, so you must go over at sufficient speed to ensure that you can balance reasonably well, and with your arms firmly controlling the 'bars.

8. DO NOT STEER WITH YOUR HANDLEBARS WHEN YOU ARE ON THE SLOPE! Your back wheel is, by definition very light in this condition, and you can use your feet and torso to push the wheel to one side

Above: Preparing for a two-wheel hop turn: rider keeps his balance by dropping speed and adopting the standing position . . .

Above: A split-second before the bike loses all forward momentum, the rider moves his body into the turn. Too much lean, and he will lose control of the bike . . .

or another. Make a tiny hop with both feet, and "float" the wheel back to the desired side. As you are doing this, your front wheel remains pointed straight down the hill, and only when you have landed pointing in your new direction do you turn the 'bars accordingly.

9. You must use the front brake skillfully throughout the descent, easing way off just before the front wheel gets to the bottom of the descent, or to any other potential wheel traps.

Long Dropoffs

Long, steep dropoffs are dangerous, and should be approached with extreme caution. All of the techniques mentioned for short dropoffs are applicable, but the taller the hill, the greater the danger of losing control of your descent speed. What happens if you are just barely keeping your speed in check with your very best brake control – and then the descent gets just a little bit steeper? The next thing you know, you'll be going way too fast, and sideways at that, because you grabbed the back brake lever too hard in the excitement.

If you do find yourself in this predicament, usually the best thing to do is to lay your bike down on the uphill side and try to cut the speed. If the hill has a smooth runout at the bottom, you might just be able to survive coming off the hill with more speed than you planned on; but if the runout is sharp or obstacle-ridden, getting off the bike on the

Above: Initiating a front hop turn by preparing to wheelie. Correct foot position is vital.

Pulling back on the handlebars and pushing down on the outer grip to spin the bike around.

Above: Pulling up on the toe-clips and handlebars, the bike is lifted clear of the ground. Making the most of this short time in the air is vital . . .

The rider combines the vertical travel of the bike with his body's angular momentum to turn the bike about its axis, landing in a new direction.

high side might be a less dangerous option.

Whatever the nature of the descent, if things are getting out of control, you have to decide what you are going to do VERY QUICKLY. On any descent, while you think, you are gaining velocity. Remember: if in doubt, walk down!

TIGHT CORNERS: ON THE FLATS AND ON THE HILLS

When you are riding on hiking trails or any other trails on steep terrain, you are going to be faced with many tight corners. These are often too tight to navigate in a normal riding manner, and they often occur, rather inconveniently, on the steepest hills. Either you learn the tricks necessary to turn very tightly, or you get off every time you approach such a corner.

To turn a tight corner, you have three options:

1. Hop the front wheel around.
2. Hop the rear wheel around.
3. Hop both wheels into the air and spin the bike to face the desired direction.

The correct choice depends on:

1. How much room you have: if you can ride slightly beyond the line that you will be leaving on, then a front wheel hop will line you up with the original position of your back wheel. This maneuver works especially well on uphill **switch-backs**.
2. The position of any obstacles: if you have no room beyond your de-

THE FRONT HOP TURN

On entering, the rider prepares for a wheelie.

A downward push on the outside handlebar helps spin the bike around.

On landing, dynamic traction is used to accelerate away.

sired line of departure, a rear wheel hop works well, particularly on downhill switchbacks.
3. What line you need to take out of the corner.

The two-wheel hop is the basis of most trials maneuvers, allowing you to turn about your center AND to move in any direction on level, uphill or downhill trails.

No matter which hopping technique you choose, you will have to overcome one serious drawback: you have lost your forward momentum. You will only be able to get started again if you can give a mighty **dynamic weight transfer** heave. You can also help yourself by putting your rear wheel on a relatively flat spot when you land it.

For a rear wheel turn, the rider digs the front wheel into the corner and locks the brake . . .

As the rear wheel hops upwards, the rider initiates the rotation with his shoulders and hips . . .

Staying upright through good use of downward force, landing impact absorbed by sinking down.

LARGE OBSTACLES: LIVING FOR LOGS

Mastering large obstacles is one of the greatest challenges and pleasures of mountain biking. It takes a fair amount of nerve to charge an obviously unyielding and immovable object such as a boulder or log, as well as a certain degree of self-control. Most novice riders attempt to surmount such obstacles by simply smashing into them, as if such actions will somehow scare the object and cause it to miraculously shrink away. In reality, the only thing to shrink will be the biggest chainwheel on the bike, several expensive teeth at a time!

Brute force is not the answer; you must subtly float over such obstacles. It's all a matter of timing, and it will take a lot of practice to get it right, so it would be wise to remove your two largest chainwheels while you are learning this technique. You will also be making things easier for yourself if you can find large, partially-buried logs on which to practice. When you are ready, here's what to do:

1. Approach the obstacle (in this case a log) from 3 bike-lengths away in a 26-inch (66-centimeter) gear, at a slow-but-not-too-slow speed. Your saddle should be right down lest the descent on the far side of the obstacle turns out to be one that you will always remember!

2. Roughly one wheel diameter away from the log, accelerate hard, lifting the front wheel off the ground. As you accelerate, and while you are still pedaling, sink down onto your legs just a bit as if you are about to spring. In fact, you are.

3. Your last pedal stroke is the one that places the front wheel atop the log; stop pedaling with cranks horizontal (relative to the bike). Don't let

CROSSING LARGE OBSTACLES

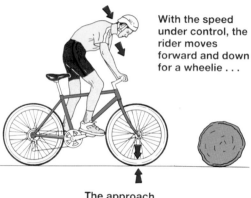

With the speed under control, the rider moves forward and down for a wheelie . . .

The approach

Pulling back on the handlebars produces a wheelie . . .

The wheelie

For the best result, the leap must be made just after the front wheel makes contact with the log. Wait too long, and the rear wheel will smash into the side of the obstacle . . .

When the rear wheel makes contact with the log, the rider starts to sink down, and gradually moves his body weight to the rear . . .

Rear wheel contact

your body lag behind: your head must be over your handlebars when the front wheel is on the log.

4. Place the front wheel neatly at the 11 o'clock position on the log. Almost immediately, you uncork a mighty leap and push forward on the handlebars. Your rear wheel should skim up the face of the log without touching it until the rear tire alights at the 10 o'clock position. Your leap should occur very, very shortly after you place your front wheel on the log; if you wait too long, your rear wheel will slam into the log, killing your momentum.

5. Since you have pushed forward on the handlebars, with your body atop the log, you are in the perfect position to roll down the other side of the log – way, way back. On descents from very large obstacles, you should be able to feel your saddle touching your breastbone!

6. You descend with light pressure on both brakes, having had two fingers on each brake lever the whole time.

What can go wrong?
● If you don't raise your front wheel high enough and it rams the obstacle, you can bend your forks. This can happen when there is poor grip on the approach to the obstacle.

● If you let your body hang back, your rear wheel will slam into the face of the log, and you won't make it over.
● If your saddle is still raised, it will push you onto your face during the descent.

Remember: good obstacle-leaping is a matter of timing and practice. Listen for any sounds of impact as you perform the maneuver – if you are doing it right, you shouldn't hear any!

Overleaf: Practice hard, and you could be as good as this rider.

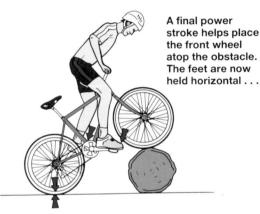

A final power stroke helps place the front wheel atop the obstacle. The feet are now held horizontal . . .

Front wheel contact

The rider springs upward and pushes forward. The rear wheel starts to rise . . .

Pushing up

With his weight now at the rear, the front wheel is now much lighter. Its descent is under control, and its impact with the ground is softened . . .

Front wheel descent

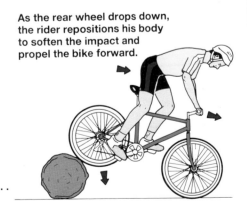

As the rear wheel drops down, the rider repositions his body to soften the impact and propel the bike forward.

Rear wheel descent

CHAPTER 5

ADVANCED RIDING TECHNIQUES: FAST DESCENTS

Since the dawn of mountain biking, fast descents have been an addiction for many riders. Indeed, mountain bikes evolved for high-speed downhills, replacing the "paperboy bikes" that had begun to show their limitations. Beloved and even craved, such descents can also prove fatal. Many riding areas where mountain biking flourished early on have subsequently been closed off, due mainly to conflicts between cyclists descending trails at speed and other, more sedate users such as hikers and horse-riders. It is important that you understand and appreciate the negative sides of high-speed riding (**Chapter 8** deals with the ethics of mountain biking, including the right and wrong areas for fast descents), as well as the exhilaration they offer. In short, SUCH DESCENTS CAN HURT YOU, AND THEY CAN KILL OUR SPORT.

The best place for exploring high-speed riding is in an officially sanctioned race on a closed and patrolled race course. If you like to ride fast, don't be shy about entering such races; you don't have to be first over the finishing line to have a good time, but you can still satisfy your need for speed in the best possible way. Such races also provide an excellent way to learn more about mountain biking: you will be guaranteed to learn more from one well-run race than from a month of recreational rides.

So how do good riders and racers manage to descend hills so rapidly? As in low-speed riding, there are a few basics which will help you learn to descend quickly and in control. The first of these is to choose the right terrain on which to practice:

1. Find a hill that is moderately steep, good in length and with plenty of width (if there is such a treasure in your locale!). This hill should not be:
- Frequently used by hikers.
- Driven on by cars or trucks.
- Used by horses and their riders.

2. In order to reduce the risk of serious injury, you should ride UP the hill BEFORE trying to descend it, ensuring that there are no closed gates, new trenches, rockslides or surprise jeep parties.

3. Wear your helmet, gloves, protective eyegear and even your knee and shin pads.

4. Need I mention stretching again?

GOING STRAIGHT

Riding a mountain bike down an absolutely straight dirt/gravel/ rock/ sand/mud road or trail is difficult enough without the added consideration of corners, so lets leave corners aside for now. How do you go fast in a straight line on a rough surface, on a bike with essentially no suspension? In a word, you relax. If you tighten up because, say, you are frightened, your bike will not appreciate it. Your bike is quite capable of descending a hill with very little help or advice from you. All you need to do is to make gentle "suggestions" now and again about the line that you would like to follow, and to use the brakes when necessary to avoid building up excessive speed. So just relax.

Now lets consider your eyes. On a fast descent, you should look straight ahead: not too far, but not too close. If you look out too far, you will hit obstacles close to you; but if you concentrate on the area immediately ahead of your front wheel, you will get into wild weaving as you try to avoid obstacles that you don't see in time. I like to focus on the area about 2 or 3 seconds riding ahead,

For many mountain bike riders, fast descents are what it's all about. The exhilaration of a high-speed run is unbeatable.

using my peripheral vision and frequent glances further ahead to warn me of potential problems further out. If you remember nothing else, remember this:

NEVER LOOK AT AN OBSTACLE; LOOK AT THE CLEAR PATH. YOU HIT WHAT YOU LOOK AT!

Your body has a natural tendency to subconsciously steer in the direction of vision; so if you look at a tree, chances are that you will ride into it. So always keep your eyes focused on the chosen line of descent.

While on the subject of eyes, there are several good reasons for wearing protective eyegear. A bug or a stone, or even just thick dust in your eye can cause you to lose vision for too long in BOTH eyes. Wind in your eyes can also be a problem, causing your eyes to water with such severity that you can lose clear vision. If you do have a problem with your eyes while descending at speed, chances are you will crash with disastrous results.

Those of you who wear eyeglasses have a real advantage here, but for those of you who don't, it's not too late to run out and snap up some fashionably expensive designer bike eyewear!

Vibration

A mountain bike at speed on rough ground vibrates a lot. After a long descent, a rider's hands and arms can be numb from all the shaking, let alone the stress from near-constant braking. You can ease the strain on your hands and arms by doing the following:

• Check your tire pressure: if you are running 70 or even 45 PSI in your tires, you're being beaten to death. Your tires are your suspension. Forget about your forks, unless you have a flexible stem or soft bars – your tires are what count. The lower their pressure, the more isolated you and your arms will be from road shock . . . until you let the pressure drop too low and end up with a

A rider travelling at speed with everything right: eyes focused on the path ahead; arms relaxed; good hand-grip; good positioning of the upper body.

puncture due to a pinched tube. Your lowest safe tire pressure is, unfortunately, a matter of experience and a function of your weight, how fast you go, and how often and how hard you hit obstacles. Some riders go as low as 25 PSI, but you must determine your own best pressure.

• Loosen your grip: most novice riders suffer from the dreaded "tight grip" phenomenon. If you grip too tightly, your rapidly tiring hand and arm muscles will hinder the movement of the handlebars. You want to hold on to your 'bars just tight enough so that they aren't torn from your grasp. Pretend that your handgrips are twice their normal size, for, in a sense they are. Relax! The 'bars are going to shake with or without you.

• Consider more flexible handlebars: titanium is half as stiff as steel, but at least as strong, so a titanium bar of the same dimensions as a fine steel bar will flex twice as much under a given load. The bar becomes a spring, a suspension isolating the rider's hands from the worst of the road shock. Titanium bars are also much lighter than steel bars. Unfortunately, they are neither inexpensive nor widely available. Another approach is the suspended or isolated stem, in which the bar is pivoted on the upright, with foam pads controlling its rotation. The stem becomes a shock absorber, able to screen out the worst of the vibrations coming up from the road. Both approaches reduce the levels of vibration by a noticeable extent, but they can't eliminate them entirely. You still need to be loose as a goose!

Suspensions

Why not design suspensions for mountain bikes? The problem with suspensions is that they need to be stiff in order to avoid being forced to vibrate by those massive legs bobbing up and down at 100 rpm. A suspension tuned for a comfortable ride could not cope under normal

---

Steering on the trail by turning the handlebars drains energy. This rider makes good use of his upper body movements, allowing him to steer with weight shift.

pedaling excitation, so suspensions for bicycles need to be much stiffer than, say, that of a motorcycle. Weight is also important – some attempts at suspension design have added too much weight. One exception is the Moulton suspension, clever rubber suspension of minimum weight. It is simple, effective and reliable, and ride comfort at speed on a rough hill is noticeably improved. Other suspensions are sure to be perfected soon – the need is too great to be ignored.

EFFECTIVE BRAKING

Hill descents make bikes accelerate. If you don't brake on a hill, you will end up going faster and faster until you are out of control. In order to avoid the undesirable byproducts of excessive speed (loss of control, violent impacts, and injury to your person), you must brake in order to hold your speed in check.

Braking at speed on a descent is an art, and an art that must be practiced gently. It is best done with gentle applications of both brakes, with emphasis on the rear unit. You aren't trying to decelerate, you are

Shock-isolation for a rider's hands and arms is an important factor on fast descents. One solution is titanium handlebars.

simply trying not to accelerate. Consequently, the dreaded weight-shift isn't such a problem, and your rear brake unit will retain most of its effectiveness.

Brakes get hot if left locked on for long periods, so try to cycle your brakes on and off as often as possible. If you are careful and gentle enough, you can sometimes drag one brake while the other cools, alternating between front and rear every few seconds. Also, by riding with your palms slightly lower than might feel natural, you can minimize arm fatigue while braking. This position will take the braking forces through the palms of your hands rather than through the hooks of your thumbs.

GEAR CHANGES

Few descents do nothing but descend. If your all-out downhill run suddenly turns into a short but steep climb, and you are still in a 50–13 gear, you're history. Large amounts of time will be lost as you try to find a workable low gear, while other riders are passing you as if you were nailed to the hillside. You have to look far enough ahead to be able to anticipate changes in grade, so that you can shift gears at the right time. SHIFT BEFORE YOU GET THERE. DON'T WAIT UNTIL IT'S TOO LATE! When the descent resumes, shift back up

The last thing you want while making a fast descent is some grit, or an insect, caught in your eye. Wraparound visors help avoid such dangers.

(sometimes it is best to use the front, chainwheel derailleur for small changes in grade). A burst of power can be a life-saver for a biker, and you can't apply power if you are still in a 26–10 gear and coasting. Stay in control of your speed, and stay in the right gear as you accelerate.

Finally, DON'T SCREW AROUND AT SPEED – IT COULD KILL YOU, SO TAKE IT SERIOUSLY.

TAKING CORNERS AT SPEED

If you have been descending a long, straight hill at high speed, you'll probably have to lose some of that "Vitamin S" for any tight corners. Braking into a tight corner uses the same braking principles that you learned in **Chapter 4**:

• You must rely on your front brake.
• Try not to slide either wheel.
• Position your body weight as far back as you can.

Right: Hurtling round a corner; but with the brakes covered and body weight shifted well back, this rider is in full control.

Taking the corner smoothly, eyes "reading" the course a short distance ahead.

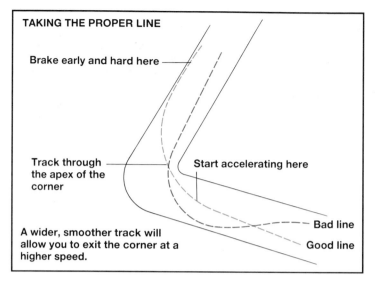

TAKING THE PROPER LINE

Brake early and hard here

Track through the apex of the corner

Start accelerating here

Bad line

Good line

A wider, smoother track will allow you to exit the corner at a higher speed.

the most force BEFORE they slide; a bike travelling sideways isn't slowing down as quickly as a bike **tracking** under the control of skilled braking.

It is best to brake early, so that you are free to accelerate under power through the apex of the corner. The best line around the turn often depends on the terrain features in the corner – you don't worry about some theoretical "best line" if there is a large boulder sitting on it. In general, you want to make the corner as large as possible by coming in wide, cutting the apex tightly, and coming out wide. The larger you make the radius, the faster you can go. Try to look as far around the corner as you can, giving yourself time to find a quick line that avoids any obstacles.

Many riders slide BEHIND the saddle during this hard braking effort to counteract the forward weight shift, and retain the effectiveness of the rear brake.

If you have neglected to maintain your brakes, or if you have overheated them on the descent, this is where you will find out about it. Good riders can **downshift** while

they are braking hard, using their thumbs for the shift levers, and two fingers for the brakes – practice this skill.

Some riders like to cut their speed by pitching their bikes sideways into the corner, but this is less effective than a controlled and skilled application of the brakes on most surfaces. Remember: tires generate

High-sides
Most fast riders would agree that the quickest way through a corner is to track through with minimum sliding. If you are sliding, you can't apply the power so easily after the apex of the corner. Sliding a corner is also riskier than tracking through – if you catch a rock or a pothole while hanging out, you may become a flying

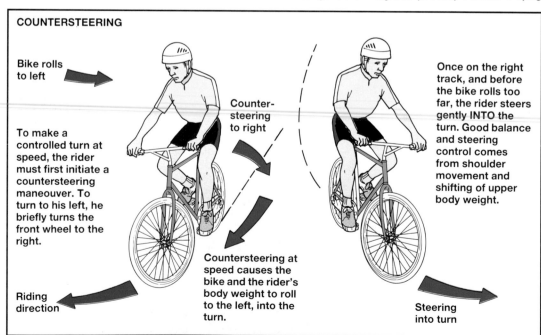

COUNTERSTEERING

Bike rolls to left

To make a controlled turn at speed, the rider must first initiate a countersteering maneouver. To turn to his left, he briefly turns the front wheel to the right.

Countersteering to right

Counter-steering at speed causes the bike and the rider's body weight to roll to the left, into the turn.

Riding direction

Once on the right track, and before the bike rolls too far, the rider steers gently INTO the turn. Good balance and steering control comes from shoulder movement and shifting of upper body weight.

Steering into turn

particle in your own right. This form of suborbital launch is called a "high-side", and is a favorite of racing motor-cyclists.

Countersteering

Few riders can explain how they initiate a turn. Turning is counter-intuative: to turn left, you must first turn right! This is called countersteering. At speed, your handlebars don't really control your direction as much as they control your **roll rate**. To turn to the left, you need to lean to the left. But if you turned the handlebars to the left at the start of the turn, the bike would roll . . . to the right! If you turn briefly to the right, the bike will roll to the left, and keep rolling until you bring the 'bars back to the left to stop the roll.

So, coming into a left turn, you briefly turn to the right until you have leaned to the left the correct amount. Then you relax and let the bike find its equilibrium. Once established on the right arc through the corner, you should again steer and balance by shifting your shoulders, not by tugging on the 'bars.

Countersteering is very powerful, and all riders do it, even if they don't know it. You can get into a corner a lot faster if you understand the principles of countersteering, so try it!

Blind Corners

When entering a blind corner, call out or ring a bell. It's your responsibility to avoid hitting anyone or anything else coming around the corner. Unless you are on a trail or road that you know to be absolutely free of other users, your speed on entering such corners must be low enough to allow you to take evasive action or stop. If you blast through blind corner and hit somebody, you, and all other mountain bikers, are in big trouble.

So save your serious speed for closed race courses, and only go fast on open trails when you can see that the coast is clear.

Below: Extra stability for this rider as he speeds through a corner, his leg acting as an "outrigger".

Overleaf: Correct body position puts enough weight on the front tire for balanced cornering.

CHAPTER 6

COMPETITIVE RIDING

If you want to learn to ride your mountain bike to your full potential AND get the most enjoyment while doing so, one of the best ways is to compete. Just as there are many types of mountain bikes, so there is a wide range of mountain bike competition, from the slow and precise to the fast and wild, with a full range in between. You can try all of the forms of competition, or concentrate on specific events that suit your style and personality. If there are no such events in your area, there's no reason why you can't take the initiative and begin organising them yourself!

OBSERVED TRIALS

Observed Trials, also known as Trial-sin, is one of the most popular forms of off-road mountain bike competition in the world. Derived from similar motorcycle events, the basic idea is to ride through a short segment of difficult terrain (called a "section") without either foot touching the ground in the process. The sections, of which there are usually ten, are marked with red and blue ribbon, and are linked by a designated trail to form a loop. A rider will usually complete this course three times for a total of thirty stages. The wide range of rider's skills makes it almost impossible for organisers to accommodate all riders in one set of sections. The best trials organisers will split the entry into classes based on riding skill (and sometimes by equipment), and will offer separate sections for the beginners and experts. It usually takes at least four classes to handle the spread of abilities, and that's without considering any separate classes based on rider age and sex.

Speed is unimportant, it's accuracy that counts. With that in mind, it's standard practice for a rider to

Observed Trials competition offers a tremendous challenge to mountain bike riders. A good, varied competition can be held on a small area of land just about anywhere.

Above: High up in the mountains, a Technical Trail competitor comes up against a problem forming part of a highly demanding rocky trials section...

Above: A welcome "catch" from a spectator as he tries to get out of trouble with a wheelie. He also picks up 5 penalty points as a result of the spectator's action.

by the section's "Start" sign and the opposing ribbon, he or she is officially in the section and under official scrutiny. As the rider negotiates the obstacles, the checker watches closely, ready to penalise for infractions such as leaning on a tree or straying out of bounds. Dabbing a foot is also penalized as follows:

- One point for one dab.
- Two points for two dabs.
- Three points for three dabs.
- Three points also for four dabs.
- Five points for five dabs – the same penalty incurred for riding out of bounds or crashing.

Clubs and sanctioning bodies differ in their interpretation of "dabs" taken when the rider is not moving forward: some will add five penalty points for a static dab, others only one point. The current trend is to follow the international rules and allow dabs while the bike is motionless. Whatever the rule, the designated checker marks each rider's scorecard with a hole-punch after he or she has completed the section. The best a rider can do in a typical thirty-section Trialsin event is zero points – and the worst is 150 points (five points per section, ten sections per loop, three loops) for complete failure in every section!

Trialsin bikes

Stock mountain bikes can be seen at Observed Trials events, but most serious competitors ride specially designed machines with 20-inch (51-centimeter) wheels, **bashplates**, a single, low gear and special powerful brakes.

SCORE CARD 501

NAME Bob Fangwally

CLASS Novice   NO. 18

SCORE	SECTION NO.		SCORE
0 ● 2 3 5	1	7	5 3 2 ● 0
0 1 2 ● 5			5 3 2 1 ●
0 1 2 3 ●			5 3 2 1 ●
0 1 2 3 5			5 3 2 1 0
0 ● 1 2 3 5	2	8	5 3 2 1 ●
● 1 2 3 5			5 3 2 1 ●
0 ● 2 3 5			5 3 2 1 ●
0 1 2 3 5			5 3 2 1 ●
0 1 2 3 ●	3	9	● 3 2 1 0
0 1 2 3 ●			5 3 2 1 ●
0 1 2 3 ●			5 3 2 1 0
0 ● 2 3 5	4	10	5 ● 2 1 0
0 1 2 ● 5			5 3 ● 1 0
0 1 ● 3 5			5 3 2 ● 0
0 1 2 3 5			5 3 2 1 0
0 1 ● 3 5	5	11	5 3 2 1 0
0 1 2 3 ●			5 3 2 1 0
0 1 2 3 ●			5 3 2 1 0
0 1 2 3 5			5 3 2 1 0
● 1 2 3 5	6	12	5 3 2 1 0
● 1 2 3 5			5 3 2 1 0
0 1 2 3 ●			5 3 2 1 0
0 1 2 3 5			5 3 2 1 0

0's 11   1's 5   2's 3   3's 3   5's 8

ARRIVAL TIME ___   PENALTY ___

TOTAL PTS 50   TOTAL CLNS 11

PLACE 3rd

Right: Trialsin riders are just as at home on felled tree trunks as on rock outcrops. Good balance and a steady nerve are essential ingredients for success.

Below: Despite the penalty, the rider presses on to the end of the section. A good Trialsin course usually has 10 sections.

walk through each section ahead of the actual ride. He or she will look for the best line through and over the obstacles, and also take note of potential traps – slippery roots, soft surfaces, mud etc.

Each rider carries a scorecard, which is handed to the designated checker stationed at each section prior to tackling the course. As soon as the front axle of the rider's bike crosses an imaginary plane formed

Left: Having worked his way up the rock face, a Trials rider prepares for the descent, altering direction with a front wheel hop.

Above: Caught between a rock and a hard place, this rider has to produce a very powerful hop to lift his bike out of trouble.

The 20-inch wheel is used on the vast majority of special trials bikes for two reasons:

1. European rules require this wheel size – a fact that helped force the Europeans to develop the all-conquering hopping riding style. Wheels of this size don't roll easily in broken terrain, thus favoring a riding style which places them vertically on appropriate landing spots.

2. Tires for these wheels can be constructed with thick rubber sidewalls and a soft rubber tread just like scaled down motorcycle trials tires. Such tires offer phenomenal grip on rock, hard dirt, and wood – far better than any regular mountain bike tire, and weigh only 5 pounds (2.3 kilograms) per pair. A tire built like this in a 24- or 26-inch (61- or 66-centimeter) size would be far too heavy for any practical use.

It can honestly be said that there are no effective trials tires available in the larger sizes. But on the down side, the 20-inch wheel has an extremely high rolling resistance on anything but the hardest of surfaces, and the "scaled-down motorcycle trials tire" tread patterns currently in vogue on the best trials tires clog

horribly in mud, and become almost useless in wet clay. In such circumstances, the large diameters and widely-spaced, self-cleaning tread patterns of regular mountain bike tires have the advantage, making trials bikes with larger wheels more competitive in slippery conditions.

Hopping and rolling

Since the maturation of the hopping style in trials riding (perfected in

Europe during the mid-1980's and since adopted worldwide), the definition of a challenging obstacle for an expert trials rider has changed dramatically. Not only can the experts make some very impressive vertical leaps; they can also use the hopping technique to slowly and carefully step up and over obstacles far too large to clear in one leap. The best riders feel at home balancing on either wheel, and can execute powerful leaps from either position.

Steep drops, which trials riders would have once tried to ride down, are now jumped down: the rider will bounce up to the edge on the rear

Left: For all the skill that is involved, accidents are waiting to happen, so wearing sufficient protective gear is a wise move. Bikes can be protected from the obstacles by fitting bashplates.

Right: It looks dangerous, but this rider's method of descent from the dropoff is safe. His bike has been custom-built to soak up this sort of punishment time and time again.

wheel, then leap to the bottom, absorbing the shock with a combination of body motion and skillful use of the brakes.

Many riders use the **skidplates** fitted to their bikes as hooks: approaching a sharp-edged obstacle, the rider will often deliberately land on the skid plate, balance briefly, and then heave the bike the rest of the way up the obstacle, thus reducing the magnitude of the leap necessary.

As spectacular as the hopping technique may be, it consumes vast quantities of energy, and those who depend on the technique all of the time will tire quickly. The best trials stylists know to hop only when the terrain makes it absolutely necessary. The rest of the time they will roll. For a time, European trials bikes were fitted with ludicrously short crank arms under the theory that trials riders hopped everywhere and anywhere, and that the presumably better balance and descending capabilities afforded by the shorter cranks was worth a loss of up to 25% in torque. Fortunately, this trend has been reversed, and the modern trials bikes now usually come equipped with longer crank arms, offering a more useful split between hopping balance and rolling power.

Whatever your bike and preferred riding style, Trialsin riding is tremendous fun, and perhaps the best and quickest way to improve your bike-handling skills. Everybody who rides a mountain bike off-road would benefit from entering the occasional trials competition. If there are none held near you, lay out a course for yourself! Invite your fellow riders and have an unofficial event, using the scorecard shown in this Chapter as a guide. Most trials organizers, myself included, started laying out our own trials courses because there were simply none around. In fact, designing and marking trials events can be just as rewarding as actually riding in them.

Under the close scrutiny of the designated section checker, a Trials rider takes on a potent combination of wood and water.

RACING

If the challenge in Observed Trials riding lies in finding the answer to the question: "Can I ride my bike from A to B?", the challenge of Racing lies in finding the answer to the question: "Can I ride from A to B – and beat everyone else?" A mountain bike race is not the place to stand still on one wheel – it's all about speed.

Such organized races are the best, if not the only places to ride flat-out, uphill and down, in an off-road environment. These events come in many forms, and there is bound to be a type of race which will suit your temperament, experience level and equipment.

Downhill races

In this, the Grandfather of all styles of mountain bike racing, the format is simple and straightforward: one rider at a time races against the clock, trying to descend a dirt track as fast as possible. Not surprisingly, such races are characterised by great speed, high levels of adrenalin and equally high levels of risk. But if you feel the need for speed, a downhill race is THE event for you. At a well-run event the course will be closed to other traffic, with corner workers and emergency medical personnel standing by. Pre-running the course is usually allowed, so that each rider is familiar with the corners and surface features – surprises aren't always a good thing when travelling at high speed.

There are two main factors affecting a rider's downhill speed:
1. Ability to read the terrain.
2. Ability to take corners.

When pointed downhill, some riders simply go faster. Heavier riders have a distinct advantage in such situations because the force pushing a downhiller along is proportional to his or her mass. But skill also plays its part in fast tracking, as the rider taking the smoothest line will lose the least energy through bike-bouncing. For the best downhillers, the secret lies in a mixture of good

Right: Fast downhill racing is most definitely not for novices. A rough surface, steep gradient and tight corner all in one will prove a hard enough test for the most experienced of riders.

Below: The ability to ride fast is not enough to make a good downhill racer. The rider must have the descent under total control while pushing body and bike to their limits.

eyesight, a relaxed riding style to help maintain control, and lots of experience.

However, the big rider eventually pays a price when it comes to taking corners. Corners are the "resistors" in the circuit, the inhibitors to flat-out speed. Very fast cornering puts a tremendous load on a mountain bike's tires, pushing the rubber to the limits – and beyond. The cornering load on the already overworked tires will only increase if the rider happens to be well-built, thus canceling out to an extent the large rider's downhill straightline speed advantage.

The tires can be helped in their

frantic search for grip if the rider has developed good terrain-reading skills. Small, almost imperceptible changes in the terrain can be used to advantage, enhancing a rider's cornering power and speed.

Cross-country racing

This is perhaps the most common form of mountain bike racing, and is similar to the familiar road-racing events in both format and physical demands. It doesn't require large

hills, nor does it always involve the tremendous speed and danger of the downhill events. Cross-country races typically take place on a 5- to 15-mile (8- to 24-kilometer) course, with groups riding a different number of laps according to their ability and experience. Such races are mass-start events, usually with the different classes on the course at the same time, but with staggered starts.

Cross-country races can be endurance events lasting several hours, and the best racers are tremendously fit athletes. Many courses are long enough that simply surviving one lap is enough of a challenge for most riders, nevermind any attempt to ride fast. A good race should offer a variety of terrain, with some single track, but most of the course run on wider dirt roads and trails to make passing safer and easier. Steep climbs and descents are welcome, with some courses famed for climbs of several thousand feet.

The key in entering your first cross-country race is to concentrate on finishing. Don't try to race the other riders; ride at your own pace, and don't worry about where you finish. Just finish! There will be plenty of races in which to improve on your speed, but getting that first race under your belt will let you know exactly which aspects of your riding skills and fitness need to be worked on.

The course

A good cross-country race course should be wide enough to allow passing over most of its length, but this is something that is not always possible. If the latter is true, getting a good starting position becomes all the more important. If your position is bad, you may find yourself stuck irretrievably behind a long line of slower riders, with no real chance of making a move. In theory, a slower

Cross-country races are mass-start events, but the course is usually narrow and difficult to pass on. As a result, getting a good starting position can make all the difference when it comes to finishing higher up the field.

rider should always move over to allow a faster competitor to pass, but things don't always work out that way in practice. Clearly, if you are a fast rider, you should start near the front of the pack. A good race organization will try to arrange the starting order by class, but YOU are responsible for finding the best starting niche within your category.

Passing on the inevitable narrow sections of trail is always a difficult maneuver. The masters in the art of passing have the ability to come up behind you, and then, before you know it, they are ahead of you. Good passers always manage to be in the right gear at the right time, and they always pay attention. When a passing opportunity arises, they are ready, willing and able to make the most of it.

Should you find yourself behind a slower rider, call out "track!". If the rider doesn't respond, shout again. If there is still no response after several attempts, do what you have to do to get by without putting anyone at risk.

Race preparation
A good warm-up before the start of a race is vital. A well-stretched and

Most cross-country races are low-speed affairs, resulting in little in the way of serious damage to riders and bikes alike.

warmed-up rider will be able to attack the course right from the starting gate, with much less discomfort during the first quarter hour's racing.

The warm-up session should consist of a half-hour's riding; starting off gently and finishing with enough effort to work up a sweat, finishing shortly before the race commences. Timing it right is important: finish the warm-up too early, and you will be in a worse condition than if you hadn't done any warm-up at all, especially on a cold, wet day.

SHORT-COURSE RACES

A short-course race is simply a mountain bike race held on a course that measures a few miles or less. These courses can be set up in city parks, or in urban areas not offering long-course possibilities. Such races are wonderful spectator attractions, for the same reasons that road racing events are so popular: the action is nearly continuous, and there is almost always something to watch.

Short courses might include some paved road, grassy lawns, a dart into an old gravel pit, a blast down an abandoned gravel road etc. As with cross-country races, these are mass-start events, but an advantage of the short length of a single lap is that less capable riders can be included, unlike the more challenging and longer cross-country race courses.

Cross-country races are a supreme test of a rider's stamina and skill. The winner of such a race has every right to celebrate.

DUAL SLALOMS

Mountain bike racing owes a lot to the sport of skiing. We have borrowed the Downhill race concept and the ski area, and in recent years we have incorporated the concept of the slalom as well. In a dual slalom event, two courses approximately equal in length are laid out side-by-side on an impressive slope. Slalom gates borrowed from skiing events are used to define each course. Two

Right: Out of the start gate – and it's quite literally downhill all the way for this Dual Slalom racer. Spectacular to watch, let alone take part in, Dual Slaloms are very similar to ski slalom events.

mountain bike racers leave the gate at the same time, each trying to beat the other to the bottom of the hill.

The rules are very similar to those in a ski slalom race: you can't miss a gate, but you can whack the gate with your 'bars, for instance. This is a "**fast twitch**" sport – great endurance is not needed here. Pedaling is minimal, since gravity on such steep slopes easily drives you faster than you want to go. Not surprisingly, dual slalom racing is wildly popular with spectators and racers alike.

HILLCLIMBS

There are two kinds of hillclimb events:
1. Those in which the hill is com-

pletely rideable, and the winner is the rider who can climb it in the fastest time.
2. Those in which the hill is almost impossible to climb, and the winner is the rider who makes the most progress up the hill.

The first type of hillclimb (similar to the American motorcycle type of climb) is growing in popularity, while the second type (more of a time trial) has always attracted riders.

The former is an extension of a challenge frequently faced by tech-

Left: Turning around one of the Dual Slalom marker poles, this competitor just manages to avoid contact and heads on downhill.

Right: The tight positioning of Dual Slalom gates on the course can keep speeds down to a point where the inevitable tumble isn't too serious for this competitor.

Below: Dual Slaloms are one of the most popular forms of mountain biking competition with riders and spectators alike.

Above: Protection for the eyes is often essential to counter any grit or dust thrown up by the bike immediately ahead.

Left: Competitors in time-trial hillclimbs are often started one at a time. On long climbs, such events are a gruelling test of mental and physical strength.

nical trail riders, namely the "unclimbable hill". Riders attack the hill one at a time, the winner being the rider who progresses the furthest up the hill. These "technical" hillclimbs always require all-out anaerobic effort on the part of the rider, though this will only last for a matter of seconds. The standing dynamic traction technique is also absolutely vital, as is an ability to accurately "read" the surface of the hill.

In contrast, riders taking part in a time-trial event set off one at a time up an inclined dirt road. Some such climbs rise several thousand feet and take each rider the best part of an hour to complete. During this time they get no rest, staying right on the anaerobic threshold all the way up the hill. It's a strenuous business to say the least!

Both types of event are quite safe since speeds are low, and both are physically extremely challenging.

Another test of a mountain bike rider's skill and imagination in the form of bicycle limbo. A supple body is essential.

These events often form part of a multi-race event held over several days, in conjunction with cross-country and downhill races, and observed trials events.

OTHER NON-RACING FORMS OF COMPETITION

Enduros

Enduros are another mountain bike sport borrowed from our motorized brethren, attracting riders who might not be interested in racing flat out, but who still like a bit of competition in the woods. An enduro takes its entrants over a marked course just once – but that course can involve a mixture of paved roads, dirt tracks, easy and difficult trails, steep hills and cross country. While the course is marked with arrows or signs of some kind, each rider is responsible for paying attention and not missing such markers.

Various segments of the course are assigned an average speed, and each rider must try to adhere to this average because there are a number of known and unknown checkpoints located around the course at which each rider's time of arrival will be recorded. The riders set off at precise times in groups of one to three, each carrying a number keyed to their start time. The aim is to arrive at each checkpoint at a specific time. To arrive early or late incurs penalty points.

Eating up a relatively straight and smooth part of an Enduro course – but what surprises lie ahead for the competitors?

The degree of difficulty of an enduro can be controlled by choosing a combination of a difficult course and a high average speed. Such a combination makes an enduro similar to a cross-country race, while an easier course and a slower average speed will highlight a rider's ability to maintain an accurate pace over varied terrain.

An enduro course often includes what can only be described as "challenges". For instance, the marked course may take the riders through a nasty bog, or maybe through a pig pen (with the farmer's permission). The sky (and good taste) is the limit on just what can be included.

Bicycle Polo

Mountain bikes are excellent substitutes for horses when it comes to this sport. The rules are very similar to those in equine polo, but expenses are much lower.

Mountain Bike Tossing

This should appeal to the Scots in the audience: take your old, battered and nearly useless mountain bike – and see how far you can toss it! This event has become a popular addition to many multi-day mountain bike events in the United States. It's a fast twitch type of event, requiring little in the way of endurance (or sobriety), so a wide range of entrants can get in on the fun!

Cheaper and smaller, but just as effective, the mountain bike is an excellent mount for a game of horseless polo.

CHAPTER 7

MOUNTAIN BIKE TOURING

Bicycle touring is about freedom – freedom to go wherever your legs will take you: down little-travelled backroads; through quiet villages; up imposing mountain passes. Places and routes that can't be fully appreciated as you rush by in a car, if a car can negotiate such routes in the first place. Bikes offer the tourist versatility, and none more so than the mountain bike. Properly equipped, they are the ideal "pack mules", rugged enough to carry heavy loads and stable while doing so. Best of all, the freedom of bicycle touring is greatly enhanced by the fact that support equipment can be removed to reveal your original mountain bike underneath it all! You are now free to explore OFF-road as well as on.

A smooth ride
The fundamental feature which makes mountain bikes so desirable for touring are the large, strong, relatively low-pressure tires which characterize the breed. They offer tremendous load-carrying capabilities and a smoother ride than more traditional touring bike tires, albeit at a small increase in rolling resistance. They are also less prone to puncture because they run at lower inflation pressures, making it easier for the rubber to flex away from the cutting object, and they often run on thicker rubber.

Choosing the right type of panniers to suit your touring needs is important. If you plan a lot of off-road touring, "high-rider" panniers are best.

An important benefit resulting from this relative impenetrability is obvious when the only route to your destination is a busy two-way road without a bike lane. Riding on such roads with all the other traffic can lead to some close calls, or even death. But with a mountain bike, you can simply drop off of the road and ride on the verge until conditions improve, or a new route can be found. Those fat tires also act as a very effective suspension, obliterating the numbing vibrations from

Whatever style of panniers you choose, always make sure they are securely attached to your bike. Loose panniers can cause you to lose control and crash.

crushed rock-surfaced roads, and smoothly passing over potholes and cobblestones.

Panniers
One of the great attractions of touring on a bike is the sense of independence it offers the rider, and most tourists choose to take their food, clothing and lodging with them as they travel. Choosing the right support equipment is a key factor in making your tour less traumatic and more enjoyable, and at the top of the list is the choice of panniers.

Panniers are the obvious and critical items which transform a mountain bike into an effective touring bike. Many of the annoying problems which arise on long tours originate in

Left: When it comes to touring, the mountain bike is extremely versatile. Belongings can be transported in panniers and removed on arrival, revealing your original off-road machine.

Right: The off-road capabilities of the mountain bike allow riders to explore areas of great beauty, without causing damage to the environment.

A good-quality mountain bike can carry surprisingly heavy loads but make sure that your belongings are evenly distributed inside the various panniers.

A valuable addition to the main panniers is a handlebar bag. These are smaller but readily accessible while in motion, and are also easily removed from the bike. They are convenient places to carry wallets, cameras and other valuables, and, because of their relatively small size, you can easily detach the bag and take it with you when you stop en route. A handlebar bag is also useful during the non-touring bulk of the year, giving you some storage space when, presumably, you will not have your panniers fitted.

The art of packing

Packing your gear into the panniers and handlebar bag is a real art, and a subject of interminable discussion among experienced mountain bike tourists. There is one golden rule to follow to make things easier: **Always assume that the insides of the panniers will get wet in most touring areas.**

With that in mind, all of the contents should be grouped into "families", and each family should be wrapped inside its own plastic bag. In turn, each packing space within the pannier should be lined with, say, a plastic garbage bag. Once this is done, you should be able to ride through all but the heaviest of downpours with peace of mind.

the fundamental design features of the panniers, so some thought and research is important before you hand over your money.

Firstly, consider the type of riding you are likely to undertake: will you always be on roads, or will you venture onto narrower, off-road tracks and trails? If you never plan to leave the security of a prepared roadway, then you would be wise to

choose front panniers of the "low rider" style. But if you are likely to occasionally follow an off-road route while your bike is loaded up, low rider panniers can be a problem, snagging on every obstacle at trailside. For these situations, "high rider" front panniers are a better choice, though at the cost of a higher payload center of gravity.

The type of riding you plan to undertake should also play a part in your choice of side- or top-loading panniers. The former are very convenient to load and unload when your bike is stationary, and even more so if they have been removed from their mounting racks altogether; but it's a different story if you are trying to get hold of something packed inside while actually riding! Top-loaders are easier to gain access to while on the move, but they don't offer the ready access of the side-loaders when lying on the ground. Your choice of which type is best for you should be made on the basis of the relative frequency with which you will need to get into the bags while cycling, or at the end of the day when the bags have been removed from the bicycle.

Right: For those longer, more ambitious trips, mountain bikes can be carried on a car roof-rack. Securing and removing the bike is quick and simple.

USING PANNIERS CORRECTLY

Make sure the pannier support racks are firmly attached to your bike frame.

The panniers in turn should be securely attached to the racks. Loose panniers can make your bike unstable.

Use any built in straps to stop the pannier contents from shifting as you ride.

Move the heavier items within the panniers as far forward as possible to improve front wheel traction.

Attach each pannier as far forward and as low as possible to enhance steering and stability; but make sure there is no interference with your pedaling action.

Pack the contents sensibly, allowing quick and easy access to items you intend to use frequently.

FOOD FOR THOUGHT

Carry lightweight, freeze-dried food for your main meals

Try to buy fresh local produce whenever possible

Eat healthy, high-energy items (dried fruit, cereal bars etc.) while out touring

Don't eat big meals while out riding. Try to derive your energy from several small snacks.

Avoid rich, fatty foods as much as possible – they could disrupt your touring plans!

Just what goes into each pannier varies from rider to rider, but it is wise to try and keep the contents as lightweight as possible, even though a well-equipped mountain bike can carry up to 90 pounds (41 kilograms) if pressed. Less weight is always better, especially when it comes to off-road touring, and you can make things easier on yourself through careful choice of the food you carry while riding. If you intend to tour through a populated area, plan on buying most of your provisions locally. On the other hand, if you are riding in a remote area, you will need to stock up with typical backpacking food which is light and non-perishable.

Clothing

Clothing is another important area requiring some research beforehand. Basically, you don't want to carry heavy clothing when you positively don't need to – but then weather in many parts of the world is unreliable at best. Don't assume that just because it is "always" nice in the area you intend to visit at a specific time of the year, that it will be so when YOU go there. Take enough warm clothing and rainwear

Right: If he can find a shallow enough point, this rider will be able to ride over the river bed with ease.

Overleaf: The view might be spectacular, but carry a puncture kit just in case.

just in case things are anything but typical weather-wise. The answer lies in layers of clothing. Layers of wool or polypropylene with a breathable windbreaker are much more comfortable than a heavy, non-breathable waterproof suit. Although you may well end up being wet in both cases, you will probably prefer the comfort level of the former choice.

You should always reserve and preserve a set of dry clothing for use at your campsite. There is nothing quite so discouraging as coming into camp after a long day's ride in a monsoon, knowing that you haven't got a single stitch of dry clothing to put on!

After food and clothing, the next items to go into your panniers should be those necessary to keep your bike functioning. You must use your judgement as to how far you go with spares transportation: if you are about to circumnavigate Antarctica by yourself, without any support, you may want to take just about everything (including a straight-jacket). On the other hand, touring in, say, France, probably won't require that you carry your own spare

derailleurs, crank-arms, frame parts etc.

Spare tires should be joined by four spare inner tubes, thus sparing you mandatory stops for puncture-patching should the worst happen. It's much more pleasant to be able to undertake any repair work in camp at the end of the day than have to do it at the side of a road.

Another good idea is to fit extra-long shift and brake cables before you set off, so that if the end-fitting breaks off, you can simply pull some extra cable through and tie a knot to secure it.

On those epic tours to which the mountain bike lends itself so nobly, it's worth carrying some tools – just in case. Items like a hack-saw and hammer, in addition to the mandatory chain-breaker, crank-arm puller, screwdrivers, knife, and basic allen and open-end wrenches. These heavier tools can be used in conjunction with duct-tape, hose clamps and baling wire for stop-gap repairs to broken frames, and just about any other failure that can occur to a relatively simple machine like a bicycle.

Other life-saving items to carry along? Maps, for one. It's always a good idea to buy a general map of the area you intend to tour before you go for planning purposes, but try to buy more detailed maps of the local area when you are nearer to the tour site.

Carrying a First-Aid kit is always a good move, especially if it includes some insect-repellant and some talcum powder or other anti-saddle sore medications.

Finally, assume that darkness will catch up with you at some point along the route, and bring appropriate (but lightweight) lights for just such an emergency.

Right: A well-earned drink at the end of another day. Good planning and the right support equipment will help you to enjoy your tours all the more.

Below: Touring by mountain bike often allows access to areas which are off-limits to other forms of transport. Make the most of such opportunities.

CHAPTER 8

MOUNTAIN BIKING ETHICS

Imagine that you are out hiking. You are nearing the end of your first day on the trail, tired but happy and at peace as you sit resting on the rocks, looking out at the mountains. Suddenly, the peace is shattered by whoops and hollers from uphill as a group of five fast-moving mountain bikers pound around the next corner up, sliding and spraying dirt and rocks everywhere. As they speed through the area in which you are sitting, their bikes kick up a heavy trail of dust that coats you and your food. The cyclists have knocked over your backpack, and your camera (which had been resting atop the pack) has been sent sprawling in the dirt. The lens is cracked. You suddenly realize that you hate mountain bikers, and that you will not rest until they and their machines are banned from this place and all places like it.

Incidents just like this have happened all too often in real life. As a direct result, many riding areas have been closed to mountain bikers. This is the single greatest problem clouding the future of our sport. In some

What could be better than a challenging ride through some great off-road wilderness? But take a closer look at that small sign . . .

areas where mountain bikes have been common for over a decade, it is almost too late; the riders there are fighting to save the small fraction of riding areas that are still open to them. It is in those areas of the world where mountain biking is just starting to take off that hope exists – if the riders in those areas will learn from history soon enough to avoid making the same mistakes.

For those of you in parts of the world where the mountain bike is still a new phenomenon, beware of the following downward spiral which has characterised the decline of our sport in too many areas already:

• Typically, the mountain bike bursts upon the scene and is immediately adopted by those who want a new challenge, or who want to be free of the constraints of the road and go where no cyclists have gone before.

• There follows a period of exploration and experimentation, as the new bikers try riding in different areas and in different styles.

• The fast-growing riding population splits up into the racers, technical trail specialists, trials, and recreational riders. Some grow to love the thrill of speed, searching for that thrill wherever they can find it. Some of these fast riders are lucky: they live near big, open riding areas unused by horse-riders and hikers.

Above: It's a sad fact that the irresponsible behavior of a minority of mountain bikers has led to many ideal riding areas being closed off to our sport.

They practice their art with abandon, and live happily ever after. But most of the fast riders aren't so lucky: they live in or near cities, and their riding areas are also well-developed hiking and horse-riding routes. But they are young and determined, and they love to ride fast, regardless of any slower "traffic".

• At first the other users are amused by the odd, fat-tired bikes being ridden so strenuously on the hiking trails. But then the near-collisions and irritations begin to build up. Soon, murmurs of anger and concern are spreading around the hiking and horse-riding communities.

Right: It may look funny, but if our sport is to survive, we must do all we can to counter the negative image of mountain bike riders held by so many.

- Eventually, the inevitable serious incident occurs, anti-mountain biking sentiments are galvanized, and the well-organized groups mobilize against our sport.

Shortly afterwards, despite a few poorly-organized attempts at gathering public and official support for the sport, the riding areas are closed to mountain bikers. Not just to the reckless bikers, but to the technical trails riders; to the casual recreational riders; to the father who rode the easier trails with his two sons. In short, ALL mountain bikers. Soon, with the closure of other local riding areas made easier by the precedent set in the first case, more riding areas begin to close, one by one, until the nearest legal riding area is a 2-hour drive away. For most of the younger riders, there is now nowhere to ride.

A mountain biker stands out on many trails, simply because he or she is the only trail user who is travelling at speed. Hikers? Slow and reverent. Horses? Slow and ponderous. Mountain bikers? ZOOOOOOMMMM!! And that is part of the problem. Slow riders are accepted by other trail users because slow riders fit in. But if a hiker meets a hundred slow, quiet, friendly riders, and one who has a complete disregard for other trail users, it's that one individual he is going to remember. How realistically can we expect to rid ourselves of that irresponsible minority? How can we save our sport?

The Right Approach

We can start by behaving well ourselves, setting a good example to those we ride with. We need to put ourselves in the shoes of the hikers and horse-riders and learn to appreciate the fact that they too are seeking enjoyment on the trails. If we don't, in just a few years we may not have a sport worthy of its name. Right now, we all have a lot to worry about.

CODE OF CONDUCT

Here are some rules and suggestions which, if followed by all of us, would end our problems forever. It is hopelessly idealistic to assume that all mountain bike riders will follow such guidelines, but this Code of Conduct is a start:

1. Use organized races to satisfy your high-speed needs. Nobody minds mountain bikers going fast, just so long as such riding is undertaken in the right place, and race courses are the right places.

2. Find a high-speed descent practice area which is not used by hikers or horses, and get permission from the owner to ride there.

3. Never ride in a closed area. Doing so will only result in even tighter restrictions on access.

A startled horse is a danger to you as well as its rider. Let them know of your presence and pass slowly, or stop completely.

Hikers have just as much right to be on the trail as we do, so treat them with courtesy by dismounting and letting them pass by.

4. NEVER, EVER ride fast in a popular hiking or horse-riding area. If you must ride in such an area, do so in a slow and deliberate manner, keeping your speed on descents under complete control.

5. When you approach a hiking party coming your way, make every effort to yield to them. As you get nearer, pull over to the side of the trail and stop. Adopt a friendly and courteous manner; be free with directions and suggestions for good hiking destinations. If the hiking party moves off of the trail for you, slow to a walking pace before you ride past them, and thank them politely with lots of smiles.

6. When you find a horse coming toward you, don't take any chances: pull off to the side of the road or trail and stop. Horses can be unpredictable, and a horse that panics can easily injure its rider. Once again, adopt a friendly manner and wish the rider a pleasant trip.

7. If approaching a horse or hikers from behind, slow to their pace. When you are within range, call out and ask for permission to pass. When granted, wait for a wide enough area in the trail, then pass with caution at a moderate speed, thanking them for their cooperation.

8. Always obey directional signs on trails. NEVER go down an "up" trail, or vice versa – any collision that may result will be entirely your fault.

9. Do not enter a blind corner at high speed UNLESS you are competing in a sanctioned race on a closed and controlled race course. ALWAYS assume that there is a family of hikers coming the other way, and ALWAYS call out to alert anyone just around the corner.

10. Never cut switchbacks or **"free-style"** through the bush on a steep descent. We all know that you can descend steep hills, so you don't have to prove anything to us.

11. Try to avoid locking up your rear wheel. This does more damage to a trail than anything else you can do – a cyclist at speed can generate a lot more power with his brakes than by turning his pedals.

12. Don't destroy vegetation when you go trials riding. Be a little more sensitive about where you ride – flower beds and rock gardens DO NOT MAKE GOOD TRIALS SECTIONS.

13. A strong technical trail rider can easily tear up soft, muddy terrain. Try not to make a rut which could transform the trail into one long ditch once the rains come by carrying your bike over soft areas. If you are tearing up the steep surfaces, again, don't ride the trail.

14. Accord wildlife the same respect and consideration that you would give to an elderly hiker or children on the trail. You may not love animals, but other people do, and an animal lover who considers mountain bikers to be a menace can be a powerful enemy.

15. Join your local mountain bike riding area preservation group. If there isn't one, start one. I can assure you that local hiking, horse-riding, and environmental groups are very well organized.

16. Offer to help other user groups or land management bureaucracies

with trail maintenance and other chores. Become a constructive force, ready to help out.

17. If you organize a competition, consider making it a benefit event for a local charity, or even an environmental organization. It pays to win the friendship of these people!

18. Find out about, and work with your local land-management bureaucracy. Help them to establish a sensible policy on mountain biking by taking representatives riding. Point out how they could help to reduce further the friction between mountain bikers and other trail users.

If we can all live by these rules and just have a little consideration for others, we will be able to go on riding in our favorite areas. Isn't that worth slowing down for?

An alternative scenario: Just as you settle down on the trail for a bite to eat and a rest, a group of mountain bikers rides around the uphill corner at a sensible speed. On seeing you, they immediately slow down, coming to a stop a few feet away. You get into a conversation about interesting things to see on the trail, and one rider tells you about a waterfall nearby that you didn't know about. Another rider warns you about the hornet's nest they had just stumbled into. They wish you a good hike, and ride off down the trail. You are impressed by their friendly and courteous manner. They looked like they were having fun, didn't they? Pretty soon, your thoughts turn to the possibility of purchasing a mountain bike of your own.

Appreciate and understand the rights of other off-road users, and future generations of budding mountain bike riders will be able to experience the full range of thrills and spills of our sport.

GLOSSARY

aerobic exercise muscular activity which is fuelled by oxygen.

alloy a mixture of different metals (the number and ratio of which are variable), with the aim of producing an alloy with specifically improved characteristics e.g. increased tensile strength, greater resistance to corrosion etc. The most common alloy used in mountain bike frames is steel alloy: a mixture in which the majority is steel, but with quantities of vanadium, manganese and chromium added.

anaerobic exercise muscular activity occurring at such an intense rate that fuel is delivered without the utilization of oxygen. Such exercise can be maintained for only a short period of time, and oxygen is eventually required to enable recovery at the end of the period of exercise.

binder bolt used in conjunction with a hand-operated lever to tighten or loosen the seat tube within the seat post, thus allowing alterations in seat post height to be made quickly and easily. This type of bolt is also used by certain mountain bike manufacturers to allow quick and easy release of the bike's front wheel, the bolt being incorporated in the wheel hub.

cages these form the outer framework of the pedals, and surround the pedal axle. They offer the rider improved foot-grip for riding in rugged, off-road environments by means of a serrated top which grips the sole of the rider's footwear. The extent and pattern of the serrations does vary, as does the overall shape of the cage (top-line "bear trap" or "bear claw" cages sport very aggressive serrations, and are usually oval in shape). Materials used in their construction vary from metals for the higher quality items, to moulded resin/plastic for the cheaper products.

cantilever brakes the most common type of brake unit found on mountain bikes. So called because of the cantilever system containing the brake blocks either side of the wheel rim. When the rider applies pressure to the brake lever, the brake cable is pulled upwards. This in turn pulls the connecting cable linked to each brake arm up, and pushes the brake blocks onto the rim via pivot bosses. The brakes have now been applied, and the pads are in contact with the rim.

carbon-fiber "hi-tech" tightly woven or matted, resin-embedded man-made fiber reinforcement material with excellent fatigue resistance and inherent strength. It is also very expensive to work with, but its use in the construction of mountain bike frames is increasing.

cast magnesium method of forming magnesium alloy products by use of either vertical or horizontal casts.

chainwheels the large wheels attached to the right-hand crank, forming part of the gearing system in conjunction with the derailleurs, cogs, freewheel and "switchers". The wheels vary in diameter (small for low gears; medium for middle gears; large for high gears), number (three is normal, but "quad" units are available) and shape (off-round wheels are said to be better for the novice mountain biker as they get the most out of their high pedal force/low pedal speed riding style). Aluminum alloy is the most common material used in their construction. Also known as chainrings.

chrome-moly a combination of chromium (a highly corrosion-resistant metal) and molybdenum (a high-quality, heavy metal), used in conjunction with steel, sulfur, silicon, manganese, carbon and phosphorous to form a steel alloy. The addition of chromium helps improve the alloy's corrosion resistance; while the addition of molybdenum counters the effects of "temper brittleness" during heat-treatment, and "weld decay" (a side-effect caused by the presence of carbon). The resulting chromemoly steel alloy is very strong and versatile, and is used in the construction of top-line mountain bikes.

city bikes term applied to the increasing number of mountain bikes to be seen on city streets, even though the bike is, by definition, primarily an off-road machine. Major difference is in the tire tread pattern selection, which has to be geared towards comfort for the rider on predominantly smooth-surfaced roadways.

cleats strips of wood, metal or other materials fastened onto, or projecting from, footwear to strengthen grip and prevent slipping. Cleated footwear can be used in conjunction with the pedal cages to give the rider excellent grip of the pedals, as well as helping to avoid foot-slip on marginal surfaces such as mud.

cogs the series of toothed wheels located at the center of the rear wheel. On mountain bikes, there are usually between five and seven such cogs in the same number of sizes. Each cog represents a different gear setting when used in conjunction with the chainwheels forming part of the crankset. The rear derailleur shifts the chain on and off the various cogs, setting the chain down on a particular cog's teeth in accordance with the rider's gear selection up front.

composites hybrid materials produced by combining two or more types of reinforcement materials. Costs can be reduced while achieving an optimum set of properties for a specific application. These can include better heat, chemical and fatigue resistance.

dabbing placing of the foot or feet on a surface in an attempt to maintain or regain stability. Important when taking part in Observed Trials riding where dabbing (inadvertent or otherwise) by a rider on part(s) of a section will incur penalty points.

derailleurs front and rear derailleurs form part of the gearing system and drivetrain.

The derailleurs move the chain sideways, feeding it from one chainwheel or cog to another according to the rider's gear selection input through the "shifters". For high gears, the rear derailleur shifts the chain over the various cogs (usually 5, 6 or 7 in number), while the front derailleur ensures that the chain is making contact with the teeth of the largest chainwheel; for middle gears, the front derailleur is engaged to shift the chain onto the middle chainwheel; for low gears, the smallest chainwheel is engaged.

downshifting working down through the available gears. A good rider can do this smoothly, selecting the right gear at just the right moment to suit changes in terrain surface and topography immediately ahead, thus avoiding any loss of momentum caused by choosing the wrong gear at the wrong time.

dropoffs change in topography from a relatively flat route to a descent. Dropoffs vary in steepness and height, but whatever their characteristics, each one should be approached and descended with due care and attention.

fanny packs small storage pouches which are an integral part of some articles of clothing, or are separate items which can be attached behind and/or below the

saddle. Excellent for small items such as snack food, or that windbreaker you might need if the weather turns bad.

fast ride the riding style generally credited with being responsible for the development of the mountain bike. Fast ride descents on very steep descents in America proved too much for relatively flimsy road bikes; gradually new, stronger, lighter and more versatile machines – the first of the true mountain bikes – were developed to take on the descents. Today, fast downhill rides are still one of the most popular forms of mountain bike riding.

fast twitch quick-movement, quick reaction riding – always a real challenge to a rider's skill, concentration and alertness.

fat tire bikes nickname given to mountain bikes, based on the very obvious increase in tire width in comparison to the skinny tires fitted on regular road bikes. Road bike tires have a maximum width of 1.25 inches, whereas mountain bike tires start at 1.5 inches, and go up to 2.2 inches. In general, the greater the width, the better the off-road handling characteristics.

fillet brazing an alternative to welding processes as a means of joining frame tube elements without the use of lugs, and with much less heat involved. The tubes to be joined are heated, then joined by use of a brazing rod of a metal that has a lower melting point (brass is widely used). The brazing metal is allowed to run into the joint area, producing a fillet to hold the tubes together. A good fillet-brazed joint is characterized by an extremely smooth finish, and is the result of much skill on the part of the operator involved. Such frames are usually slightly heavier, but just as strong as any lugged, welded example. The skill involved in producing a good fillet-brazed joint also means that bikes sporting frames constructed in this manner tend to be higher in quality and price.

fire roads rough but eminently rideable routes in off-road areas.

freestyle a very individual, no-rules riding style.

honking a style of riding which can be used when climbing in the standing position. The aim is to make the most of the muscle power produced when the rider's body is raised immediately after each power pulse, rather than relying on the legs to transfer the body weight into a downward push on each pedal. This style of riding can be used in the vertical plane, with the rider producing short "steps"; or it can be used in the horizontal, with the rider swinging his weight from side to side in conjunction with the turning of each pedal.

indexed shifters gear-selection mechanisms with individual click-stops for each individual gear. The vast majority of today's mountain bikes are fitted with such units, although they do incorporate an element of manual override for those who prefer to set their gears by their own fine judgement.

kevlar a man-made, reinforced plastic fiber (kevlar 49 to give it its official title) that is stronger but lighter than steel. Extremely expensive, but its use in the

construction of mountain bike frames is increasing.

latissimus dorsi major muscle in the upper sides of the trunk, close to the shoulder area. Development through weight training is an important part of upper body strength improvement.

lock-up the seizing up of a wheel or wheels in difficult and desperate riding conditions. A phenomenon to be avoided if possible.

lugged joints in contrast to the straight tube-to-tube joining found in fillet-brazing and TIG-welding, lugged joints have the actual junction of the tubes concealed by covering lugs. Not the smoothest join to look at, but strong nonetheless.

lugless joints as in fillet-brazing and TIG-welding, both of which join one tube to another with the minimum of bonding material in evidence.

lycra brand name for spandex: an elastometric (rubber-like) synthetic fiber used to produce a wide range of elastic yarns used in woven and knitted fabrics and garments. A lycra/spandex product is usually lightweight, and can return to its original shape and dimensions after severe stretching (up to 600%).

pawls elements forming part of the freewheel at the core of the multi-gear cog unit within the rear wheel.

penetration protection a good strong helmet will be constructed from materials which protect the rider's head from serious injury by blocking the penetration of sharp or heavy objects such as rocks through the helmet.

pins two pins form part of each link plate in a bike chain, and form part of the bond between the inner and outer plates. By removing one of the pins with a chain link extractor, the chain can be "broken". Insertion of the pin will rejoin the chain.

polypropylene part of the plastic family, this strong fiber has a very low density and is used in the manufacture of non-absorbent, lightweight woven and knitted fabrics. A common element in waterproof riding gear.

power pulse pushing down and turning of the pedal with the rider's foot.

power stroke see **power pulse**

raised-rib street tires a tread pattern with a raised center rib, with a relatively smooth finish. Tailored for use on smooth street surfaces, although they can be used for off-road riding.

rim brakes general term covering both cantilever and U-brakes, as both provide braking power by applying the brake pads within the brake blocks directly to either side of the wheel rim.

roller small elements, two of which are included in each link plate of the bike chain. The rollers help produce the inherent flexibility in the chain, in conjunction with the pins and bushings.

rolling resistance this relates to the extent to which a tire, or the surface that the tire is in contact with, will deform at the point of contact. The roll resistance can be affected by the pressure of the tire: on a smooth road, high inflation for a hard tire is preferable to limit rolling resistance; but on a rough, rocky surface, the pressure should be reduced to give a slightly softer tire.

sawing loss of bike stability and control of the handlebars, resulting in wild arm movements which swing the handlebars and front fork/wheel unit from side to side in a desperate attempt to regain control. It doesn't work.

shifting cables the connectors running from the "shifters" to the front and rear derailleurs. Made of wire, they are carried in a protective flexible tubing to reduce exposure to damage such as chafing and severing. Also known as Bowden cables.

skidplates protective plates, similar to bashplates, which can be fitted to counter the possibility of damage to the bike under certain extreme riding conditions.

slicks nickname given to mountain bike tires optimized for use on on-road/smoother street surfaces, although they can also be used in certain off-road conditions with acceptable results. Such tires are easily distinguishable in that they lack any form of tread pattern; they have a completely smooth surface, in total contrast to the various intricate knobby tire tread patterns optimized for off-road riding. See **tread patterns** for further details.

switch-backs extreme change in route direction with users switching back to the way they came, but travelling in the opposite direction to that in which

they approached. Extreme switch-backs are also known as U-turns.

TIG-welding a process used to join bike frame tubing, using a welding electrode material in a controlled atmosphere to join the heated bare metal. TIG stands for Tungsten (the welding electrode material) Inert Gas (the controlled atmosphere of argon to protect against corrosion); this form of welding can be used on a wide range of frame-tubing materials, producing lugless joints every bit as strong as those resulting from other forms of welding or brazing. TIG-welded joints are rougher than other types, but these can be treated cosmetically with a polyester spackling compound. The process is cheaper and quicker than brazing, and is especially good on thicker frame tubing; consequently, the majority of mountain bike frames are joined in this manner.

toe-clips metal, plastic or fabric units which fasten to the front of the pedal cages, holding the front of the rider's foot for improved foot-grip and better foot

positioning. As a consequence, the rider's crank revolutions via the pedals will be more powerful and last longer through each pedal turn. A wide range of toe-clips are available, most incorporating adjustable clips or straps to secure the rider's shoe.

tread pattern a characteristic feature of the fat mountain bike tires is the distinctive raised pattern forming the upper surface of the tire itself. Though there are many different patterns and arrangements of those patterns, the general rule applied to them all is that the more knobby the pattern, the better its off-road adhesion on marginal surfaces. However, these "aggressive" treads are very poor when it comes to riding on paved surfaces; for these surfaces, tires with a smooth tread – slicks – are a better choice. The right choice is very much dependent on the nature of the terrain you intend to ride on.

twice-per-crank-revolution each pedal covers half of a crank revolution (180°) when turned by the rider's foot. Therefore, it takes two power strokes (one on the left pedal, and one on the right) to turn the crank through a complete 360° turn.

U-brakes alternative style of brake apparatus, but also based on the cantilever center-pull principle. A yoke acts as the mounting point for a pair of long brake arms which overlap at the top. Application of the brake blocks to the wheel rim is the same as that for cantilever brakes. The "U" relates to the practice among some manufacturers of mounting this type of unit in an inverted position, beneath the chainstays, to form the rear brake unit.

ulnar nerve a major nerve running down from the upper arm, supplying muscles in the forearm, hand and fingers.

welding method whereby two metal surfaces are fused together by heating them to their melting points. Welded joints can be further strengthened by the addition of a filler metal. See also **TIG-welding**.

FURTHER READING

General illustrated books
Ballantine, R. *Richard's New Bicycle Book*

Coello, D. *The Mountain Bike Manual*

Lynn, I et al. *The Off-Road Bicycle Book*

Ricketts, B. *The Mountain Biking Handbook*

Sloane, E. *The Complete Book of All-Terrain Bikes*

Sloane, E. *The All New Complete Book of Bicycling*

Van der Plas, R. *The Bicycle Touring Manual*

Van der Plas, R. *The Mountain Bike Book*

Technical manuals
Van der Plas, R. *Cycle Repair*

Van der Plas, R. *Mountain Bike Maintenance*

PHOTOGRAPHIC ACKNOWLEDGEMENTS

P.3: Allsport; **P.5**: Allsport; **P.6**: John Pratt-Pursuit Photo; **P.8**: Allsport; **P.9**: Lew Plummer (top), John Pratt-Pursuit Photo; **P.11**: John Pratt-Pursuit Photo; **P.12**: Bob Munro; **P.15**: Simon McComb Photography; **P.16–17**: Allsport; **P.18**: Lew Plummer; **P.19**: John Pratt-Pursuit Photo; **P.20**: Simon McComb Photography; **P.21**: Simon McComb Photography, Lew Plummer (bottom); **P.22**: John Pratt-Pursuit Photo (top), Simon McComb Photography; **P.23**: Simon McComb Photography; **P.24**: John Pratt-Pursuit Photo (top), Simon McComb Photography; **P.25**: John Pratt-Pursuit Photo (top), Bob Munro; **P.26**: Lew Plummer (top left & bottom right), Simon McComb Photography (top right), John Pratt-Pursuit Photo; **P.27**: Simon McComb Photography; **P.28–29**: John Pratt-Pursuit Photo; **P.30**: John Pratt-Pursuit Photo (top), Simon McComb Photography; **P.31**: Simon McComb Photography (top), John Pratt-Pursuit Photo; **P.32–33**: Allsport; **P.34**: Simon McComb Photography (top), John Pratt-Pursuit Photo (bottom), Lew Plummer; **P.36–37**: John Pratt-Pursuit Photo; **P.38**: John Pratt-Pursuit Photo; **P.39**: Allsport; **P.40**: Simon McComb Photography; **P.41**: Lew Plummer; **P.42**: Simon McComb Photography; **P.43**: Simon McComb Photography; **P.44**: Lew Plummer; **P.45**: Simon McComb Photography, Allsport (bottom right); **P.46**: Lew Plummer; **P.47**: Simon McComb Photography; **P.48**: Lew Plummer; **P.49**: Lew Plummer; **P.50–51**: Allsport; **P.53**: Allsport; **P.54**: Marin Bikes; **P.55**: Simon McComb Photography; **P.56–57**: Simon McComb Photography; **P.58**: Simon McComb Photography; **P.59**: John Pratt-Pursuit Photo; **P.60**: Lew Plummer; **P.61**: Lew Plummer; **P.64–65**: Allsport; **P.66–67**: John Pratt-Pursuit Photo; **P.68**: John Pratt-Pursuit Photo; **P.69**: John Pratt-Pursuit Photo; **P.70**: Simon McComb Photography (top), Lew Plummer; **P.71**: Allsport; **P.72–73**: Allsport; **P.75**: John Pratt-Pursuit Photo; **P.76–77**: John Pratt-Pursuit Photo; **P.78–79**: Allsport; **P.80**: Lew Plummer; **P.81**: John Pratt-Pursuit Photo; **P.82**: John Pratt-Pursuit Photo, Allsport (bottom); **P.83**: John Pratt-Pursuit Photo; **P.84–85**: Allsport; **P.86**: John Pratt-Pursuit Photo; **P.87**: John Pratt-Pursuit Photo; **P.88–89**: John Pratt-Pursuit Photo; **P.90**: John Pratt-Pursuit Photo (top), Allsport; **P.91**: John Pratt-Pursuit Photo; **P.92**: John Pratt-Pursuit Photo; **P.93**: John Pratt-Pursuit Photo; **P.94**: Allsport; **P.95**: John Pratt-Pursuit Photo; **P.96**: John Pratt-Pursuit Photo, Allsport (bottom); **P.97**: Lew Plummer; **P.98**: John Pratt-Pursuit Photo; **P.99**: John Pratt-Pursuit Photo; **P.100–101**: John Pratt-Pursuit Photo; **P.102**: Lew Plummer; **P.103**: John Pratt-Pursuit Photo; **P.104**: Lew Plummer; **P.106**: Lew Plummer, Mark Langton (bottom); **P.107**: John Pratt-Pursuit Photo; **P.108–109**: Simon McComb Photography; **P.110**: Simon McComb Photography; **P.111**: Lew Plummer, Simon McComb Photography (bottom); **P.112**: Simon McComb Photography; **P.113**: Simon McComb Photography; **P.114–115**: Simon McComb Photography; **P.116**: John Pratt-Pursuit Photo; **P.117**: John Pratt-Pursuit Photo; **P.118**: Simon McComb Photography; **P.119**: Simon McComb Photography; **P.120–121**: Allsport; **P.122**: John Pratt-Pursuit Photo; **P.123**: Simon McComb Photography; **P.124**: John Pratt-Pursuit Photo; **P.125**: Simon McComb Photography; **P.126**: John Pratt-Pursuit Photo; **P.127**: John Pratt-Pursuit Photo.

ADDRESSES

AUSTRALIA

Australian Cycling Council
153 The Kingsway
Cronulla
Sydney NSW 2230
Australia

Bicycle Federation of Australia
399 Pitt Street
Sydney NSW 2000
Australia

CANADA

Association Quebecoise du
 Velo de Montagne Inc.
C.P. 425
Haute-Ville
Quebec
Canada G1R 4R5

Canadian Cycling Association
Touring Department
333 River Road
Vanier
Ontario K1L 8B9
Canada

Vancouver Off-Road Cycling Club
1856 W. 4th Avenue
Vancouver
B.C. V6J 1M3
Canada

Whistler Off-Road Cycling
 Association
Box 796
Whistler
B.C. V0N 1B0
Canada

FRANCE

Association Francaise de
 Mountain Bike
3 Villa de Saboins
92200 Neuilly
France

VVT
6 Rue A. Moreau
93240 Stains
France

GREAT BRITAIN

British Cycling Federation
70 Brompton Road
London SW3 1EN
Great Britain

British Cycling Federation
Touring Bureau
3 Moor Lane
Lancaster
Great Britain

Cross-Country Cycling Club
5 Old Station Cottages
Ford
Arundel
West Sussex BN18 0BJ
Great Britain

Mountain Bike Club
3 The Shrubbery
Albert Street
Telford
Shropshire TF2 9AS
Great Britain

Manx Mountain Bike Club
19 St. Catherines Drive
Douglas
Isle of Man
Great Britain

The Rough Stuff Fellowship
9 Liverpool Avenue
Southport
Merseyside PR8 3NE
Great Britain

SWITZERLAND

MTB Cycletech
Muristrasse 42
CH-3006 Bern
Switzerland

UNITED STATES

Alki Bicycle Club
2722 Alki Avenue S.W.
Seattle
Washington 98116
USA

Arizona Bicycle Sports Association
PO Box 30776
Tucson
Arizona 85751
USA

Aspen Cycling Club
617 E. Cooper
Aspen
Colorado 81611
USA

Bicycle Federation of America
1818 R Street N.W.
Washington
D.C. 20009
USA

Bicycle Trials Council of the
    East Bay
PO Box 9583
Berkeley
California 94707–0583
USA

Bicycle Trials Council of Marin
PO Box 13842
San Rafael
California 94913–3842
USA

Cincinnati Off-Road Bicycle Racing
    Association
101, 710 W. Main Street
Cincinnati
Ohio 45140
USA

Concerned Off-Road Bicyclist
    Association
Box 149
15236 Victory Boulevard
Van Nuys
California 91411
USA

Dallas Off-Road Bicycle
    Association
1517 Fernwood Drive

Plano
Texas 75075
USA

Kentucky Trail Men
1103 S. First Street
Louisville
Kentucky 40203
USA

League of American Wheelman
6707 Whitestone Road
Baltimore
Maryland 21207
USA

Mountain Bike Club
2728 S. Second Street
St. Louis
Missouri 63118
USA

Mountain Bike Madness
38602 Sierra Highway
Palmdale
California 93550
USA

Mountain Magic ATB Club
27 Northeast 1st Avenue
Glenwood

Minnesota 56334
USA

Mountaintown Outdoor Expeditions
PO Box 86
Ellijay
Georgia 30540
USA

National Off-Road Bicycle
    Association
1750 E. Boulder
Colorado Springs
Colorado 80909
USA

New York City All-Terrain Cycling
    Association
Suite 4L
315 East 21st Street
New York
New York 10010
USA

Off-Road Bicyclists of Arizona
9542 E. Duncan
Mesa
Arizona 85207
USA

Portland United Mountain Bikers
2148 N.E. Schulyer
Portland
Oregon 97212
USA

Responsible Organized Mountain
    Pedalers
218 Victor Avenue
Campbell
California 95008
USA

Rocky Top Riders
PO Box 392
Oak Ridge
Tennessee 37830
USA

Southern Appalachian Mountain
    Biker Association
577 Martina Drive
Atlanta
Georgia 30305
USA

Two Wheel Drive
1706 Centra S.E.
Albuquerque
New Mexico
USA